John Sweney

Songs of redeeming love

No. 2

John Sweney

Songs of redeeming love
No. 2

ISBN/EAN: 9783337265168

Printed in Europe, USA, Canada, Australia, Japan

Cover: Foto ©Thomas Meinert / pixelio.de

More available books at **www.hansebooks.com**

SONGS

OF

REDEEMING LOVE

No. 2.

EDITED BY

JNO. R. SWENEY,   C. C. McCABE,

T. C. O'KANE,   W. J. KIRKPATRICK.

———————

PHILADELPHIA:

JOHN J. HOOD,

1018 Arch Street.

CINCINNATI:

CRANSTON & STOWE,

Chicago and St. Louis.

⊣PREFACE.⊢

THE success of SONGS OF REDEEMING LOVE, No. 1, has been so great that the editors have determined to issue SONGS OF REDEEMING LOVE, No. 2.

We send it out upon its merits, confident that it will meet with the heartiest commendations of all who use it.

Hymns new and old are found within its pages. Many hymns of the Wesleys have been selected, for no hymn book seems complete without them. There are many new pieces here published for the first time which we well know will soon be resounding in prayer meetings, revivals, and camp meetings all over the Republic. There are some pieces here that everybody must learn and must sing, simply because they cannot help it.

More than a million copies of the books made rich by the best productions of Messrs Sweney, Kirkpatrick, and O'Kane have already been sold. That fact is a sufficient comment upon their excellence.

CRANSTON & STOWE, } Publishers.
JOHN J. HOOD,

---

1 Singing of Jesus.

FANNY ANDERSON.　　　　　　　　　　　　　　JNO. R. SWENEY.

1. O I am singing of Je - sus, Hap-py as mor-tal can be;
2. O I am singing of Je - sus, Praising him all the day long,
3. O I am singing of Je - sus Songs he de-lighteth to hear;

Fine.

How can I help but a - dore him, He is so gracious to me:—
Singing his in - fi - nite mer - cy, Telling his goodness in song.
Singing, be-lieving, o - bey - ing, Waiting till he shall ap - pear.

Holding me up when I falt - er, Giving me light from his throne,
O I am singing of Je - sus, Singing his wonder-ful love;
Singing, be-lieving, o - bey - ing, This is my constant em - ploy;

Use first four lines as Chorus. D. C.

Cheering me on with his coun - sel, Keeping my hand in his own?
Singing of rest for the wea - ry, Rest in his kingdom a - bove.
He is my Strength and Redeemer, He is my comfort and joy.

3

Let not Your Heart be troubled.

T. C. O'K.   T. C. O'KANE.

1. "Let not your heart be trou-bled, Nei-ther let it be a-fraid,"
2. In heaven are man-y man-sions, He has hastened to pre-pare,
3. To us he gives this prom-ise, Bid-ding each to fol-low him,

Were words of sweet-est com-fort, By our dear Re-deem-er said.
That all his true dis-ci-ples In his end-less bliss might share.
And we thro' this way on-ly, Heav-en's gates can en-ter in.

CHORUS.

There is joy for the ransomed, Joy for the ransomed, There is

joy, endless joy for you, ... Where the saints sing forever, Near E-den's
yes, endless joy for you,

riv-er, There is joy, endless joy for you.

4 He sends his Holy Spirit,
  As the Christian's daily guide,
And gives a blessed fortaste
  Of those joys that e'er abide.

5 Then onward, brother Christian,
  Ever keep the narrow road,
Till Jesus comes to bear you
  To his heavenly abode.

4

3

Sing, My Soul!

MARTHA J. LANKTON.   WM. J. KIRKPATRICK.

1. Sing, my soul! proclaim the ho - ly rap - ture Burst-ing now from
2. Sing, my soul! the rock whereon thou standest Firm, unmoved, thy
3. Hark, my soul! from distant realms e-ter - nal, Borne in light   on
4. Look, my soul! the morrow's dawn is breaking; Hail, oh, hail thy

ev - 'ry chord of thine;   An - gel choirs, their highest numbers wak-ing,
anchored hope shall keep; He, thy Lord, still walking on the bil - low,
faith's ce - les - tial wing, Love's glad songs to thee are gent-ly waft - ed,
heaven on earth be-gun!   He,   the Lord, such heights of joy re - veal-ing,

CHORUS.

Never told the bliss of a joy like mine. Saved and redeem'd, thro' simple faith in
Calms the troubled wave like a child to sleep.
Songs that by and by thou wilt learn to sing.
Holds the blessed crown that will soon be won.

Je - sus! Now I am his, and he   abides in me; Saved and redeem'd! oh,

shout aloud the sto - ry; Hid with him forevermore my life shall be.

5

DO RE MI FA SO LA SI

Jesus is Calling You Now.

J. M. W.

J. M. WHYTE.

DUET.   **QUARTET.**

1. Why do you wait a conven - i - ent day? Je - sus is calling you now;
2. Days have gone by, and the months and the years, Jesus is calling you now,
3. Darkness is deep'ning, and oh,'tis so late! Je - sus is calling you now;

DUET.   **QUARTET.**

Why do you turn from his pleadings away? Je - sus is calling you now.
Joys have depart- ed and sorrow appears, Je - sus is calling you now.
What if the Spirit left you to your fate? Je - sus is calling you now.

DUET.

He stands at the door of your heart just now, The dews of the morning are on his brow;
The promise you made him was never kept, When down by the grave-side you mourn'd [and wept.
Escape for thy life, tarry not, O soul, Escape for thy life, you may miss the goal,

QUARTET.

He is there waiting and calling you now, O will you not come to him now?
Turn to him now and his free grace accept; O will you not come to him now?
And if you miss it, what horrors, O soul! O will you not come to him now?

6

Jesus is Calling You Now.—CONCLUDED.

CHORUS.

Will you not come to him now? Will you not trust in him now?
Come to him now, come, just now, right

Just now, right now, O hear him, he's calling you now.
now? Come to him now, trust in him now,

5   I'll Live for Him.

C. R. DUNBAR.

1. My life, my love I give to thee, Thou Lamb of God, who died for me;
2. I now believe thou dost receive, For thou hast died that I might live;
3. Oh, thou who died on Cal-va-ry, To save my soul and make me free,

CHO.—I'll live for him who died for me, How happy then my life shall be!

D.C.

Oh, may I ev - er faith-ful be, My Saviour and my God!
And now henceforth I'll trust in thee, My Saviour and my God!
I con - secrate my life to thee, My Saviour and my God!

I'll live for him who died for me, My Saviour and my God!

7

Unto the Uttermost.

Rev. F. J. SWANEY.   T. C. O'KANE.

1. Come, weary wan-der-er, burdened with sin, God is now waiting to
2. Look un-to Je-sus, your burden lay down, Cal-vary's cross is the
3. He who is all and in all un-to men Fashions your soul in his

welcome you in; Free-ly receive the sal-vation you crave, Un-to the
key to the crown; He will forgive you who others forgave, Un-to the
image a-gain, Fully redeems you from death and the grave, Un-to the

REFRAIN.

uttermost Je-sus can save. Un-to the uttermost, un-to the uttermost,

Un-to the ut-termost Jesus can save: Un-to the ut-termost,
yes, ev-en

un-to the ut-termost, Un-to the ut-termost Je-sus can save.

8

7
Crown Him.

THOMAS KELLEY.   WM. J. KIRKPATRICK.

1. Look, ye saints, the sight is glorious, See the Man of Sorrows now!
2. Crown the Saviour, angels, crown him: Rich the trophies Jesus brings:
3. Sin - ners in de- rision crown'd him, Mocking thus the Saviour's claim ;
4. Hark, those bursts of acclamation! Hark, those loud triumphant chords!

From the fight return'd victorious, Ev - 'ry knee to him shall bow:
In the seat of power enthrone him, While the vault of heaven rings:
Saints and angels crowd around him, Own his ti - tle, praise his name:
Je - sus takes the highest station: Oh, what joy the sight affords!

Crown him,   crown him;   Crowns become the Victor's brow; . . .
Crown him,   crown him;   Crown the Saviour King of kings; . .
Crown him,   crown him;   Spread abroad the Victor's fame; . . . .
Crown him,   crown him   King of kings, and Lord of lords; . . .

Crown him,   crown him;   Crowns become the Vic - tor's brow.
Crown him,   crown him;   Crown the Saviour King of kings.
Crown him,   crown him;   Spread a- broad the Vic- tor's fame.
Crown him,   crown him;   King of kings, and Lord of lords.

A Handful of Leaves.

FANNY J. CROSBY.   JNO. R. SWENEY.

1. What! sit-ting at ease when there's work to be done! The best of the
2. What! sit-ting at ease, leav-ing oth-ers the toil Of training the
3. What! sit-ting at ease, when a bur-den of care Our brother has
4. No long-er at ease we are fold-ing our hands, But, willing to

day half its cir-cuit has run; Yon orb to its zen-ith rides
vine-yard and till-ing the soil; This truth in our mind let us
borne we might help him to bear; Oh, let us be ear-nest, and
do what the Sav-iour commands, We'll work till the har-vest, then

forth in the sky; What! sitting at ease and the har-vest so nigh!
constant-ly keep, From seed that we scat-ter the fruit we shall reap.
work while we may. The Master is call-ing, a-rise and a-way.
gather the sheaves, And bring to him more than a hand-ful of leaves.

CHORUS.

Oh, look on the fields, that al-read-y are white; The Lord hath com-

mand-ed to work in the light; Be-ware lest, in-stead of the

10

bright, golden sheaves, We bring to him on - ly a handful of leaves.

9 Ah, my Heart.

Wm. J. Kirkpatrick.

DUET—Soprano and Alto.

1. Ah, my heart is heav-y-lad-en, Wea - ry and oppressed!
2. Hath he marks to lead me to him, If he be my Guide?
3. Is there di - a-dem, as mon-arch, That his brow a-dorns?
4. If I find him, if I fol-low, What's my por-tion here?

SOLO—Tenor.

"Come to me," saith One, "and coming, Be at rest, be at rest!"
"In his feet and hands are wound-prints, And his side, and his side."
"Yes, a crown in ver-y sure-ty, But of thorns, but of thorns!"
"Many-a sor - row, many-a con - flict, Man-y-a tear, man-y-a tear."

CHORUS.   *ad lib.*

"Come to me," saith One, "and com - ing, Be at rest!"
"In his feet and hands are wound-prints, And his side."
"Yes, a crown in ver - y sure - ty, But of thorns!"
"Man - y-a sor - row, man-y-a con - flict, Man - y-a tear."

5 If I still hold closely to him,
  What have I at last?
‖: "Sorrow vanquished, labor ended,
  Jordan past!" :‖

6 If I ask him to receive me,
  Will he say me nay?
‖: "Not till earth and not till heaven
  Pass away!" :‖

The Numberless Host.

F. A. B.

F. A. BLACKMER.

1. When we enter the portals of glo - ry, And the great host of ransom'd we see,
2. When we see all the saved of the ages, Who from cruel death partings are free,
3. When we stand by the beautiful river, 'Neath the shade of the life-giving tree,
4. When we look on the form that redeem'd us, And his glory and majesty see,

As the numberless sand of the sea-shore, What a wonderful sight that will be!
Greeting there with a heavenly greeting, What a wonderful sight that will be!
Gazing out o'er the fair land of promise, What a wonderful sight that will be!
While as King of the saints he is reigning, What a wonderful sight that will be!

CHORUS.

Numberless as the sand of the sea - shore, Numberless as the sand of the shore;

Numberless as the sand,

as the sand of the shore;

Oh, what a sight 'twill be, When the ransom'd host we see,

As numberless as the sand of the sea-shore.

11 Christ the Lord is King.

Fanny J. Crosby.   A. M. Wortman, M D.

1. Shout for joy, ye ho - ly throng, Christ the Lord is King; An- gel harps, the
2. Shout for joy, ye nations all, Christ the Lord is King; Crowns before his
3. He who rent the boasting grave, Christ the Lord, is King; He who lives the
4. Shout for joy, ye realms of night, Christ the Lord is King; Hail the beams of

CHORUS.

sound prolong, Christ the Lord is King. Bear the news . . . from pole to
throne shall fall, Christ the Lord is King.
lost to save, Christ the Lord, is King.
gospel light, Christ the Lord is King. Bear the news from pole to pole, Bear the

pole, ... Spread the truth . . . . from sea to sea, ...
news from pole to pole, Spread the truth from sea to sea, O, spread the truth from sea to sea,

Lo! the Prince . . . . . of life and glo - - - - ry
Lo! the Prince of life and glo - ry, Lo! the Prince of life and glo - ry

King of heaven . . . . . and earth shall be. . . . . .
King of heaven and earth shall be,   and earth shall be.

13

12   He Saves.

FRANK M. DAVIS.   John iii. 17.   E. C. AVIS.

1. Sing glo-ry to God in the highest, For wonderful things he hath done;
2. Oh! perfect redemption to sinners, The purchase of Jesus' own blood,
3. Rejoice, then, rejoice, all ye peo-ple, The wondrous transaction is done!

He so loved the world that he gave us His on-ly be-gotten dear Son.
The vil-est offend-er is pardoned, Is saved thro' the promise of God.
The life-gate is o-pen, come, ent-er, Thro' Jesus, the Cru-cified One.

CHORUS.

Hal-le-lu - jah! hal-le-lu - jah! He saves thro' the death of his Son;
Hal-le-lu-jah!   hal-le-lu-jah!

Hal-le-lu - jah! hal-le-lu - jah! He saves thro' the Crucified One.
Hal-le-lu-jah!   hal-le-lu-jah!

14

13   Not my Love.

JENNIE GARNETT.   JNO. R. SWENEY.

1. Je-sus, Sav-iour, Lord of all, At thy feet I humbly fall,
2. Je-sus, Sav-iour, King of kings, 'Neath the shadow of thy wings
3. Thanks for all thy ten-der care, Thanks for ev-'ry gift I share,
4. When to realms of end-less day Flies my hap-py soul a-way,

Prais-ing thee that I am thine, Bought with blood,—thy blood divine.
Now in per-fect peace I rest, In thy full sal-va-tion blest.
For thy grace that keeps me still, Keeps me safe from ev-'ry ill.
When I join the ransomed throng, This for-ev-er be my song:—

CHORUS.

Not my love but thine for me, From my bonds has made me free;

Not my love but thine for me, for me, From my bonds has made, has made me free;

On the mountains bleak and wild Thou didst seek thy wand'ring child.

On the mountains

15

14 Are You Drifting?

MARY D. JAMES. WM. J. KIRKPATRICK.

1. Are you drifting down life's current, Drift-ing on a dang'rous tide?
2. Down the stream of worldly pleasure Drift-ing, drifting ev-er-more
3. Heed, oh, heed the kind moni-tion! Give your aimless wand'rings o'er;

Near the rapids' fearful per-il All unconscious do ye glide?
T'ward the great unfathomed o-cean, Bound for yon e-ter-nal shore?
Cease to seek in earth your pleasure, Head your bark for heav'n's bright shore,

Down the stream of sin and fol-ly,—Heed-ing not the danger near,
Drift-ing, drifting,—going,—whither? Aim-less, purposeless;—how vain!
Take on board the skillful pi-lot, Use the oars of faith and prayer;

Drift-ing on in self-com-pla-cence, Feel-ing no remorse or fear?
To the dark and dread forev-er! What, oh, what have ye to gain?
Then you'll make the port of glo-ry, God will guide you safely there.

CHORUS.

Hark the voice . . of yonder pilot: Cease your drifting, seize the oar;
Hark the voice, the warning voice of yonder pilot: seize the oar;

16

Are You Drifting?—CONCLUDED.

Make the blest, celestial harbor, Steer your bark for Canaan's shore.

Make the blest, celestial harbor, make the harbor,

15 Yet there is Room.

T. C. O'K.   T. C. O'Kane.

1. Hast-en to the Gos-pel Feast, From the greatest to the least;
2. Hith-er come, ye poor and blind, Here a heart-y welcome find;
3. From the hedg-es and the street, Hith-er come with eag-er feet;
4. Weary wand'rers, cease to roam From your Heavenly Father's home;

CHORUS.

Every one may be a guest, "Yet there is room." There's room enough for you,
Christ hath bidden all mankind, "Yet there is room."
Christ is waiting each to greet, "Yet there is room."
All invite you now to come, "Yet there is room."

enough, O,

There's room enough for me, Yes, room enough for all, Sal-vation's free.

16 I Praise the Lord.

H. L. G.

Dr. H. L. Gilmour.
Har. by Mame P. Gilmour.

1. I praise the Lord, when full of sin A willing Saviour took me in,
2. I praise the Lord, when I was blind, And knew not where the path to find,
3. I praise the Lord I'm in the way, My prospect bright'ning ev'ry day,

And now I love to dwell with him; Oh, glo - ry, hal - le - lu - jah!
The Spir - it came, with words so kind, And pointed me to Je - sus.
And, Je - sus help-ing, I will stay, And nev - er leave my Sav - iour.

CHORUS.

Glo - ry, glo - ry to his name; Hal - le - lu - jah, Je - sus came; I

praise the Lord the Lamb was slain To save a world of sin - ners.

4 I praise the Lord, I follow on,
Obedient to the heavenly call;
I rest in Christ, my all in all,
A perfect, loving Saviour.

5 I praise the Lord, 'mid raging storm
My soul has refuge from alarm
By resting on the mighty arm
Of Jesus Christ my Saviour.

6 I praise the Lord for sweet repose
From inward fears and outward foes;
A peaceful stream of pleasure flows
When leaning on my Saviour.

7 I praise the Lord for peace within;
I praise the Lord I'm cleansed from
I praise the Lord I'm free in him; [sin;
Oh, glory, hallelujah!

17 God so Loved the World.

FANNY J. CROSBY.   John iii. 16.   WM. J. KIRKPATRICK.

Solo ad lib.

1. God loved the world so tenderly His only Son he gave, That all who on his
2. Oh, love that only God can feel, And only he can show! Its height and depth, its
3. Why perish, then, ye ransom'd ones? Why slight the gracious call? Why turn from him
4. O Saviour, melt these hearts of ours, And teach us to believe That whosoever [whose

CHORUS.

name believe Its wondrous pow'r will save. For God so loved the world that he
length and breadth Nor heav'n nor earth can know!
words proclaim E- ter - nal life to all?
comes to thee Shall endless life receive.

gave his on - ly Son, That who - so - ev - er be - lieveth in him

Should not per - ish, should not per - ish; That who - so - ev - er be-

lieveth in him Should not per - ish, but have ev - er - last - ing life.

Be Thou Faithful.

Priscilla J Owens.   T. C. O'Kane.

1. How goes the bat-tle, brother? What news a - long the line, Dost
2. How goes the bat-tle, brother? There's glory on be - fore, Though
3. How goes the bat-tle, brother? Canst look a - bove the storm? God's
4. How goes the bat-tle, brother? I hear our Lead- er's voice; It

see our ho - ly standard a - bove the ramparts shine? The
some fall by the way-side, and some are wounded sore; But
hosts are press-ing on-ward, the con - flict wax - es warm; The
rings a - bove the con - flict, it bids us all re - joice; O

foe is charg-ing on us, but God is on our side; We
midst the toil and sor - row, the cross is lift - ed high; Press
ranks of sin are break-ing, our Lead - er cheers us on: "Be
arm - ies of sal - va - tion, how great is your re - ward:— The

must not shrink from dan - ger who serve the Cru - ci - fied. The
on to faith u - ni - ted, we con - quer when we die. "Be
brave a lit - tle long - er, the day is al - most won." A-
vic - to - ry is cer - tain to those who trust the Lord; The

20

DO RE MI FA SO LA SI

voic - es of our com - rades, they ring a - bove the field; The
faithful," gasp the dy - ing—their last words whisper cheer; "Fill
bove the dust, the blood, the tears, an an - gel cho - rus rings, "Be
glo - rious voice of Je - sus, it points us on be - fore; 'Tis

cry is "No sur - ren - der, fight on and nev - er yield;" Be
up the ranks for Je - sus, and leave no place for fear." Be
faith - ful, fel - low - sol - dier, ye serve the King of kings." Be
sweet - er than the angels' song up - on the gold - en shore. Be

faith - ful, O be faith - ful, soon ends the bat - tle's strife; O

be thou faith - ful un - to death, and win a crown of life.

19 Hold the Light up Higher.

Rev. Wm. Hunter, D. D.

T. C. O'Kane.

1. Man-y souls on life's dark o-cean, Void of helm or oar, Battling
2. Like the light-house watcher, keeking Ev-'ry bea-con bright, Waking
3. Hold the light for one an-oth-er, 'Tis the Lord's command; Seize the
4. Hold the light up higher, high-er, Thousands need your aid: Throw its

with the waves' commotion, Seek a qui-et shore. Christian brother, thine the
while the world is sleeping, Wrapt in thickest night. There is many-an o-cean
ship-wrecked, drowning brother, With a manly hand; Rouse him up to life and
flash-es nigher, nigh-er, Urge, constrain, persuade: Borrow torches from the

la - bor, By the light of love, To as-sist thy er-ring neighbor
rang - er Out up-on the shoals; Friends and comrades are in danger,
ac - tion, Ply the means to save, And by love's di-vine at-trac-tion,
al - tar, Blazing like the sun, Hold them up, nor flag nor falt-er,

CHORUS. *Spirited.*

To the port a-bove. Hold the light up high-er, higher! Hold the
Save their precious souls.
Lift him from the wave.
Till the work is done.

22

Hold the Light up Higher.—CONCLUDED.

light up higher, higher! Throw its flashes nigher, nigher! You a soul may save.

20   'Enough for Me.

E. A. H.

Rev. E. A. HOFFMAN.

1. O love surpass-ing knowledge! O grace so full and free!   I
2. O won-der-ful sal-va-tion! From sin he makes me free!   I
3. O blood of Christ so pre-cious, Poured out on Cal-va-ry!   I

Fine. REFRAIN.

know that Je-sus saves me, And that's enough for me!   And that's e-
feel the sweet as-sur-ance, And that's enough for me!
feel its cleansing pow-er, And that's enough for me!

D.S.

nough for me! And that's enough for me!   I know that Jesus saves me,

Is it for Me?

F. R. HAVERGAL.   T. C. O'KANE.

1. Is   it for me, dear Sav - iour, Thy glo - ry and   thy   rest?
2. Is   it for me thy wel - come, Thy gracious "En - ter   in?"
3. O   Saviour, pre - cious Sav - iour, My heart is   at   thy   feet!
4. I'll be with thee for - ev - er, And nev - er grieve thee more;

For   me, so weak and sin - ful? Oh, shall I be   so   blest?
For   me thy "Come, ye bless - ed?" For me, so full   of   sin?
I   bless thee, and   I   love thee, And thee   I   long   to   meet.
Dear Sav-iour, I   must praise thee, And love thee ev - er - more.

CHORUS.

O   Sav - iour, my Re - deem - er! What can   I   but   a - dore?

And mag - ni - fy   and praise thee, And love thee ev - er - more?

24

Dwell in me.

MARTHA J. LANKTON.

WM J. KIRKPATRICK.

1. Dwell in me, O bles-sed Spir - it,—How I need thy help di - vine!
2. Let me feel thy sa- cred presence, Then my faith will ne'er de- cline;
3. Round the cross where thou hast led me, Let my pur - est feelings twine;
4. Dwell in me, O bles-sed Spir - it, Gracious Teacher, Friend divine;

In the way of life e - ter - nal Keep, oh, keep this heart of mine.
Comfort thou and help me on - ward, Fill with love this heart of mine.
With the blood from sin that cleansed me Seal a - new this heart of mine.
For the home of bliss that waits me, Oh, pre-pare this heart of mine.

CHORUS.

Dwell in me, oh, dwell in me: Hear and grant my prayer to thee;

Spir - it, now from heaven descending, Come, oh, come and dwell in me.

Life of Life.

JOHN S. B. MONSELL.　　　　　　　　　　　　　　・ T. C. O'KANE.

1. La-bor-ing and heavy-lad-en, Wanting help　in time of need,
2. In the land of cloud and shadow, Where no hu-man eye can see,

Fainting by the way from hunger, "Bread of life!" on thee we feed. Thirsting
Light to those who sit in darkness, "Light of life!" we walk in thee. Thou the

for the springs of waters, That by love's　e-ter-nal law From the
grace of life sup-ply-ing, Thou the crown　of life wilt give, Dead to

Strick-en Rock are flow-ing, "Well of　life!" from thee we draw.
sin　and dai-ly dy-ing, "Life of life!"　in thee we live.

　　　26

24 I'm Holding On.

JAMES NICHOLSON.   JNO. R. SWENEY.

1. Tho' weak my faith, I'm holding on; To Je-sus I am clinging;
2. I'm hold-ing on, though Satan tries To keep me from be-liev-ing;
3. While holding on by faith I see The blood of Je - sus flowing;

I feel that now the "Mighty One" Help to my soul is bringing.
But, while my soul on God relies, The blessing I'm re-ceiv-ing.
The healing stream is touching me, New life and peace be-stowing.

CHORUS.

I'm hold-ing on, I'm holding on, Fresh strength each moment gaining,

My ling'ring doubts at last are gone, And Christ within is reigning.

4 I'm clinging, clinging, holding on,
  My faith is rising higher,
  The last remains of sin are gone;
  I have my heart's desire.

5 I'm holding on, and while I make
  A perfect consecration,
  The Holy Ghost, for Jesus' sake,
  Brings in complete salvation.

25 It Cleanseth every Hour.

TOPLADY.

T. C. O'KANE.

1. O precious blood, O glorious death, By which the sin-ner lives!
2. The blood that purchased our release Now wash-es out our stains;
3. The blood that makes his glorious Church From ev'ry blemish free;
4. Guilt-y and worthless as I was, It all for me was given;

When stung with sin, this blood we view, And all our joy re-vives.
Our scar-let crimes are made as wool, No spot of sin re-mains.
And oh, the rich-es of his love, He poured it out for me.
And boldness through that blood I have To en-ter in-to heaven.

CHORUS.

Glo-ry to God, the precious blood! I feel its sav-ing power;

By faith I keep be-neath its flood,—It cleanseth ev-'ry hour.

Copyright, 1885, by T. C. O'KANE.

28

Marching On.

JENNIE GARNETT.   WM. J. KIRKPATRICK.

1. With our col-ors waving bright in the blaze of gos-pel light We are
2. Oft the tempter we shall meet, but we will not fear de-feat, Though his
3. We have gird-ed on the sword and the ar-mor of the Lord, We have
4. Soon we'll reach the pearly gate, where the blessed army wait, Soon their

marshall'd on the world's great field; great field; We are ready for the strife and the
arrows at our ranks may fly; may fly; Thro' a Saviour's mighty love more than
ta-ken up the cross he bore; he bore; Oh, the trophies we shall win, oh, the
welcome, welcome song may ring; may ring; When we lay our armor down and re-

bat-tle work of life, Ev - er trusting in the Lord our shield.
conquerors we shall prove, Shouting, Glo-ry be to God on high.
vic-tory o - ver sin, When the bat-tle and the strife are o'er!
ceive a star-ry crown, Shouting, Glo-ry be to God our King.

CHORUS.

Glo-ry to God! we are marching, marching on, Marching to a home above;

Glo - ry to God! we are marching, marching on, Happy in a Saviour's love.

Copyright, 1884, by JOHN J. HOOD.   29

Rising in the Easter Glory.

"I shall be satisfied when I awake with thy likeness."
Psalm xvii. 15.

Rev. George R. Kramer.   Jno. R. Sweney.

1. Ris - ing in the Eas - ter glo - ry At the res - ur - rec - tion light,
2. See - ing then the saints all beaming In their crowns and robes of white,
3. Viewing then the har - vest glowing In those grand, e - ter - nal rays,
4. Waiting then for Christ from heaven As the church in days of old—

Sing - ing then the wondrous sto - ry Of the love that banished night;
See - ing then our loved ones gleaming With their forms so pure and bright;
Glad - ly reap - ing then from sow - ing In these tears thro' sorrow's days,
Crowns of joy will then be giv - en, We will walk the streets of gold—

Shall we mur-mur at the sleeping Till that great ef - ful - gent day?
Meet-ing them beyond the sigh - ing In that home be-yond the gloom,
Shall we then be heard re - pin - ing, Tho' the seed in earth remain?
We will find no cause for sad - ness That we part - ed—that we died;

Will it be a cause for weeping When our tears are wiped a - way?
Shall we grieve because of ly - ing In the dark and si - lent tomb?
Wav - ing in that morning's shining Will be seen the gold - en grain.
All shall be in per - fect gladness With the Psalmist—sat - is - fied.

Rising in the Easter Glory. —CONCLUDED.

CHORUS.

I shall be sat - - isfied, I shall be sat - - isfied, When I a-
I shall be sat - is - fied, *I shall be sat - is - fied When I a-*

wake . . . with thy like - ness; I shall be sat - - isfied, I shall be
wake with thy likeness, thy like - ness; *I shall be sat - is - fied,*

sat - - isfied When I a - wake . . . with thy like - ness.
I shall be sat - is - fied When I *a - wake with thy likeness, thy like - ness.*

28 **Asleep in Jesus.** Tune,
LAWRENCE, L. M.
pp *p* W. J. K.

1. Asleep in Jesus! blessed sleep, From which none ever wake to weep,
   blessed sleep, *none wake to weep,*
2. Asleep in Jesus! peaceful rest, Whose waking is supremely blest,
3. Asleep in Jesus! oh, for me, May such a blissful refuge be, *a refuge be;*

A calm and undisturbed repose, *sweet repose,* Unbroken by the last of foes.
No fear, no woe, shall dim that hour, *joyful hour,* Which manifests the Saviour's power.
Securely shall my ashes lie, *safely lie,* And wait the summons from on high.

From "Goodly Pearls," by per.

Tell it to Ev'ry Sinner.

CHAS. J. BUTLER.   WM. CHURCH, JR.

1. Christ on the cross atonement made, Go, tell it to ev-'ry sin-ner; With
2. In death he bowed his thorn-crowned head, Go, tell it to ev'ry sinner; But
3. His hand can break sin's slavish chains, Go, tell it to ev'ry sin-ner; He
4. This great salvation's full and free, Go, tell it to ev-'ry sin-ner; The

his own blood the price he paid, Go, tell it to ev'ry sinner. Where Justice laid its
rose in triumph from the dead, Go, tell it to ev'ry sinner. With bleeding hands, with
speaks, the prisoner pardon gains; Go, tell it to ev'ry sin-ner. To souls in sorrow's
tidings spread o'er land and sea, Go, tell it to ev'ry sin-ner. The lost, by sin so

heavy blows, Fresh from those wounds his blood still flows.
                                        [To sinners thus his love he shows, Go,
love untold He opened mercy's gates of gold, To all his glories he'll unfold, Go,
deepest night He brings sweet peace and heav'nly light,
                                        [Dark shadows quickly take their flight, Go,
deeply dyed, May in Christ's blood be purified, And safely cross death's mystic tide, Go,

CHORUS.

tell it to ev-'ry sin-ner.   Go, tell it to ev-'ry sinner, On land and

ocean wave, How Christ on the rugged cross has died, Has died the lost to save.

Peace.

Rev. E. Corwin.

T. C. O'Kane.

1. God kind- ly keepeth those he loves Secure from ev'ry fear; From the
2. What peace he bringeth to my heart! Deep as the soundless sea; How
3. How calm at even sinks the sun Beyond the clouded west! So,

eye that weepeth, O'er one that sleepeth, He gent- ly dries the tear.
sweetly singeth The soul that clingeth, My lov- ing Lord, to thee.
tempest driv- en In - to the ha- ven, I reach the longed-for-rest.

CHORUS.

As flows the river calm and deep, In silence t'ward the sea; So

calm and deep,

flow- eth ev - er, and ceas-eth nev- er, His boundless love to me.

SRL—2C 33

31 In the Secret of His Presence.

Rev. Henry Burton, M. A.

Jno. R. Sweney.

Moderato.

1. In the se-cret of his presence I am kept from strife of tongues;
2. In the se-cret of his presence All the darkness dis-ap-pears;
3. In the se-cret of his presence Nev-er-more can foes a-larm;
4. In the se-cret of his presence Is a sweet, un-bro-ken rest;

His pa-vil-ion is around me, And with-in are cease-less songs!
For a sun, that knows no setting, Throws a rainbow on my tears.
In the sha-dow of the Highest I can meet them with a psalm:
Pleasures, joys, in glorious ful-ness, Making earth like Ed - en blest:

Storm-y winds his word ful-fil-ing, Beat without, but can-not harm,
So the day grows ev-er light-er, Broad'ning to the per-fect noon;
For the strong pa-vil-ion hides me, Turns their fier-y darts a-side,
So my peace grows deep and deeper, Widening as it nears the sea,

For the Master's voice is stilling Storm and tem-pest to a calm.
So the day grows ev-er brighter, Heav'n is com-ing, near and soon.
And I know, whate'er be-tides me, I shall live be-cause he died!
For my Sav-iour is my Keep-er, Keeping mine and keep-ing me!

In the Secret of His Presence.—CONCLUDED.

CHORUS.

In the se - - cret of his presence Jesus keeps, . . I know not how;

In the secret of his pres-ence   Jesus keeps, I know not how, I know not how;

In the sha - - dow of the High-est   I am resting, hiding now.

In the shadow of the Highest, In the shadow of the Highest,

---

32   Forever with the Lord.

JAMES MONTGOMERY.   Tune, VIGIL, S. M.

1. "For - ev - er with the Lord!"   A - men, so let   it   be!
2. Here in the   bo - dy   pent,   Ab - sent from him   I   roam,
3. "For - ev - er with the Lord!"   Fa - ther,   if 'tis thy   will,
4. So, when my lat - est   breath   Shall rend the veil   in   twain,
5. Knowing   as   I   am known,   How shall   I love that   word,

Life from the dead is   in that word, 'Tis im - mor - tal - i - ty.
Yet night-ly pi†ch my mov-ing tent   A day's march nearer   home.
The promise   of that faithful word, E'en here to   me ful - fil.
By death I shall   es-cape from death, And life e - ter - nal   gain.
And oft re - peat be-fore the throne, "Forev - er with the   Lord!"

35

33 Until Ye Find.

Rev. E. H. STOKES, D. D.
Luke xv.
JNO. R. SWENEY.

Andante con espress.

1. A - las! a - las! a wayward sheep Had wandered from the fold, Par
2. He sought with many-a footstep sore, From early morn till night; Thro'
3. How long, O Lord, must I still go? How long search for the sheep? They've

o'er the mountains rough and steep, Where howling tempests rolled; The
rock - y wastes, where torrents roar, —All pathways but the right; Then
wandered far a - way, I know,—Discouraged, lo, I weep: How

Shepherd, with a burdened mind, Went forth the missing one to find, The
cried, with sad and burdened mind, The missing I have failed to find, The
long thus go, with burdened mind? "Go," Jesus saith, "until ye find;" The

miss - ing one, far, far a - way, The miss - ing one to find.
miss - ing one, far, far a - way, A - las! I've failed to find.
miss - ing one must not be lost,— Go, seek un - til ye find!

CHORUS.

Go, seek un - til ye find; Go, seek un - til ye find; The

Chorus to last verse:—
Joy! joy! the lost is found; Joy! joy! the lost is found; The

Until Ye Find.—CONCLUDED.

miss - ing one must not be lost,—Go, seek un - til ye find.
miss - ing one, no long - er lost, The miss-ing one is found.

4 I've sought my friends for many-a day,
   Have prayed for many-a year;
Yet, still they wander far away,
   O'er mountains dark and drear;
How long thus seek with burdened mind?
   "Seek," Jesus saith, "until ye find;"
The missing one must not be lost,—
   "Go, seek until ye find!"

5 Lord, at thy word I go again,
   Believing I shall find:
I listened, and a low refrain
   Came to me on the wind;
Led by the sadly joyful sound
   I rushed, and, lo, the lost was found!
Joy! joy! O blessed joy divine!
   The lost one I have found.

34 Trustingly.

H. BONAR.   WM. J. KIRKPATRICK.

1. Trust - ing - ly, trust - ing - ly, Je - sus, to thee Come I; Lord,
2. Peace - ful - ly, peace - ful - ly Walk I with thee; Je - sus, my
3. Hap - pi - ly, hap - pi - ly Pass I a - long, Ea - ger to

lov - ing - ly, Come thou to me! Then shall I lov - ing - ly,
Lord, thou art All, all to me; Peace thou hast left to us,
work for thee, Ear - nest and strong; Life is for ser - vice true,

rit.

Then shall I joy - ful - ly walk here with thee, Walk here with thee.
Thy peace hast giv - en us; So let it be, So let it be.
Life is for bat - tle, too, Life is for song, Life is for song.

35 Trusting Jesus, that is all.

EDGAR PAGE.

JNO. R. SWENEY.

1. Sim - ply trusting ev - 'ry day; Trust - ing, though a stormy way;
2. Bright-ly doth his Spir - it shine In - to this poor heart of mine;
3. Sing - ing, if my way is clear; Pray - ing, if the path is drear;
4. Trust-ing as the moments fly, Trust - ing as the days go by,

Ev - en when my faith is small, Trust - ing Je - sus, that is all.
While he leads I can - not fall, Trust - ing Je - sus, that is all.
If in dan - ger, for him call— Trust - ing Je - sus, that is all.
Trust - ing him, whate'er be - fall— Trust - ing Je - sus, that is all.

CHORUS.

Trusting him while life shall last, Trusting him till earth is past—

life shall last,

earth is past—

Till with-in the jas - per wall— Trust - ing Je - sus, that is all.

jas- per wall—

From "Gems of Praise," by per.

38

36 **The Anchor Holds.**

"Which hope we have as an anchor of the soul, both sure and steadfast, and which entereth into that within the vail."—Heb. vi. 19.

MARY D. JAMES.   WM. J. KIRKPATRICK.

1. Christ Je-sus is my anch'rage ground, No firmer ev - er can be found;
2. The storms may rage, the billows roll, The watery deep surround my soul;
3. The clouds are pierced by faith's strong eye, It sees the sun above the sky,
4. And when we've gained the heav'nly shore, Our voyage ended, storms all o'er,

And, anchored here, I   cannot fail To ride in   triumph ev - 'ry gale.
Their surging billows, mountain high, But lift me near - er   to the sky!
And tells the tem- pest-beaten soul Of rest, where billows nev- er   roll.
We'll sing our triumph in his name,—The Lamb,—thro' whom we overcame.

CHORUS.

With-in the vail my anchor's cast, It holds! it holds   a- mid the blast!

With-in the vail my anchor's cast, It holds! it holds a- mid the blast!

No Other Refuge.

JENNIE GARNETT.   WM. J. KIRKPATRICK.

1. Troubled in heart and spir - it, Je - sus, I come to thee;
2. O - ver the cold, dark mountain, Soft - ly I heard thee say:
3. Troubled in heart and spir - it, Burdened with anxious fears,
4. Troubled in heart and spir - it, Saviour, to thee I come;

Hast thou a word of wel - come? Hast thou a smile for me?
None from the door of mer - cy Ev - er were turned a - way.
Je - sus, be - hold me kneel - ing, Bath - ing thy feet with tears.
Now to thy fold I hast - en: Take the poor wanderer home.

CHORUS.

I have no oth - er ref - uge, No oth - er place to go;

On - ly thy blood can wash me clean, And make me whiter than snow.

38 Trusting Only Thee.

LOUDON FREEMAN.

T C. O'KANE.

1. Je - sus, I will trust thee When across my soul, Like a fearful tempest,
2. Je - sus, I will trust thee; There is none beside; In thine arms of mercy
3. Jesus, I will trust thee, Trust thee even now, Trust thee when the death-dew

Doubts and fears shall roll; When the tempter cometh, Surely he will flee,
I will ev - er hide; And for my ac-cept-ance, This my on - ly plea,
Gathers on my brow; Trust thee in the sunshine, Trust thee in the shade,

REFRAIN.

When I tell him, Je-sus, I am trust-ing thee. Trust - - ing on-ly
Je - sus died for sinners, Jesus died for me.
With thy precious shelter, I am not a - fraid. Je - sus, trust - ing,

thee, Trust - - ing on - ly thee, Trust -
trusting on - ly thee; Je - sus, trust - ing, trusting on - ly thee; Blessed Je - sus,

ing only thee, Jesus, my Redeemer, trusting only thee.
trust - ing, trusting on - ly thee,

41

39 I will Tell it to Jesus my Lord.

J. M. W.

J. M. Whyte.

1. When times of tempta - tion bring sadness and gloom I will tell it to
2. When out on the hill-tops, a - way from all sin, I will tell it to
3. When wea - ry with toil- ing and read - y to faint, I will tell it to
4. When darkness is dimming my path to the sky, I will tell it to

Je- sus my Lord; The last of earth's treasures borne out to the tomb, I will
Je- sus my Lord; When joyous and happy the sunshine within, I will
Je- sus my Lord; He nev - er re - fus - es to hear my complaint, I will
Je- sus my Lord; When helpers shall fail me and comforts shall fly, I will

tell it to Je - sus my Lord. This earth hath no sor- row For to-
tell it to Je - sus my Lord. To know I'm for - giv - en Is a
tell it to Je - sus my Lord. I'll cheer- ful - ly bear it, When I've
tell it to Je - sus my Lord. Though blurred my life's pages By my

day or to-morrow, But Jesus hath known it and felt long ago, And when it comes
foretaste of heaven, And Jesus is dearer to me than before, Such peacefulness
Jesus to share it, His yoke it is ea- sy, his burden is light, When life becomes
sin and its wages, He's yesterday, now, and forever the same, I'll not be for-

o'er me, And I'm tempted so sorely, I will tell it to Je-sus my Lord.
fills me, Such an ecstasy thrills me, I will tell it to Je-sus my Lord.
dreary, And I'm footsore and weary, I will tell it to Je-sus my Lord.
saken, Tho' my life should be taken, I will tell it to Je-sus my Lord.

CHORUS.

I will tell it to Je - sus, to Je - sus my Lord,
I will tell it to Jesus, I will tell it to Jesus, I will tell it to Jesus, to Jesus my Lord,

I will tell it to Je - sus, I will tell it to Je-sus my Lord.
I will tell it to Jesus, I will tell it to Jesus,

40 Num. vi. 24-26. **The Lord Bless Thee.** W. J. K.

A blessing for use in closing Sabbath-school, or other service, in the absence of a minister.

The Lord bless thee, and keep thee: The Lord make his face shine upon thee and be
[gracious

unto thee: The Lord lift up his countenance upon thee, and give thee peace. Amen.

43

41 True and Faithful.

PRISCILLA J. OWENS.   WM. J. KIRKPATRICK.

1. Ev -'ry day my soul is hap - py, For I feel my Saviour near;
2. Ev -'ry day, tho' storm and sorrow Dark-ly round my pathway rise,
3. Ev -'ry day my home is hap - py, For with Je - sus I a - bide;
4. Ev -'ry day my hopes grow brighter, Tho' the hopes of earth are gone;

'Tis his presence makes my sunshine, And his love destroys my fear.
I am look - ing up for com - fort, Far beyond earth's changing skies.
Drinking from the liv - ing fountain, With his good- ness sat - is - fied.
Ev -'ry day my rest draws nearer, As my Sav - iour leads me on.

CHORUS.

I am con - tent . . . . with thee, O my Sav - iour, I have re-
I am con-tent

solved . . . thy will shall be mine; Keep me faith - ful,
I have resolved

rit.

true and faith - ful; Fill my soul . . . with love di - vine.
Fill my soul

44

Jesus is Good to Me.

Rev. E. H. Stokes. D. D.

Jno. R. Sweney.

1. I love my Saviour, his heart is good, He has loved me o'er and o'er;
2. He calls, I rise, and he maketh me whole,—How fond his tender embrace!
3. I want to love him with all my heart, Tho' all its powers are small;
4. He's good to me in my sorrow's night, He's good in the tempest's roll;

He sought me wand'ring, I'm saved by his blood, And I love him more and more.
He cleanses and keeps me and blesses my soul'—My day the smile of his face.
I will not keep from him any part, For he is worthy of all.
He bringeth from darkness into light,—With joy he filleth my soul.

CHORUS.

Je - sus is good to me, ... Je - sus is good to me; . . . .
to me, to me;

So good! so good! Je - sus is good to my soul.

43 The World is Growing Better.

Rev. John O. Foster, A. M.

Jno. R. Sweney.

Moderato.

1. The world is growing bet-ter, No mat-ter what they say, The
2. We mark the stead-y foot-falls, We hear the tramping host, The
3. The Bi-ble cause and missions, The church and Sunday-school, The
4. O for an in-spir-a-tion To thrill the mighty throng, And

light is shining brighter In one refulgent ray; And tho' deceivers murmur, And
lines deploying widely, Encompass all the lost; And while the gospel banner Floats
steady flow of money, To keep the coffers full, While thousands of young converts Re-
bugle note of triumph, A gospel wave of song, A deeper ob-ligation T'ward

rit. *a tempo.*

turn an-oth-er way, Yet still the world grows better, And better ev'ry day.
over all the way, We'll shout, the world grows better, And better ev'ry day.
joice and sing and pray, We know the world grows better, And better ev'ry day.
what we ought to pay, And give to God the glory, Far better ev'ry day.

rit.

The World is Growing Better.—CONCLUDED.

CHORUS.

'Tis grow - - - ing, grow - - - ing, Bet - ter and
'Tis grow-ing, grow-ing bet - ter, grow-ing, grow-ing bet - ter,

bet - ter ev - 'ry day; Yes, 'tis grow-ing, grow-ing bet - ter,
ev -'ry day 'tis grow-ing bet - ter, grow-ing bet - ter, 'Tis grow - - - ing,

grow - ing bet - ter, Bet - ter and bet - ter ev -'ry day.
grow-ing, growing bet - ter, grow - ing bet - ter ev -'ry day.

44   Cassady.

CHORUS.

The righteous they are march - ing, And Je - sus bids them come!
D.C.—To wel-come travelers home, . . . To wel-come travelers home,

D.C.

And the an-gels they are wait - ing To wel-come travelers home.

1 O FOR a thousand tongues to sing
  My great Redeemer's praise;
The glories of my God and King,
  The triumphs of his grace!

2 My gracious Master and my God,
  Assist me to proclaim,
To spread thro' all the earth abroad
  The honors of thy name.

3 Jesus! the name that charms our fears,
  That bids our sorrows cease,
'Tis music in the sinner's ears;
  'Tis life, and health, and peace.

4 He breaks the power of cancelled sin,
  He sets the prisoner free;
His blood can make the foulest clean,
  His blood availed for me.

45 God's Holy Church Shall Triumph.

FANNY J. CROSBY.   JNO. R. SWENEY.

1. Press on, press on, ye workers, Be loyal, brave, and true: Great things the Lord is
2. The walls of leagued oppression To dust shall fall away; The sword of truth e-
3. Behold her marching onward, In ma- jesty sublime, A- long the rolling

doing, And greater things will do; His arm-y, still increas- ing With
ternal No power on earth can stay: Though all the hosts of darkness Were
prairies That bound our western clime; And soon from every hamlet On

each revolving year, Shall send a shout of rapture forth That all the world shall hear.
marshalled on the field, The church of God would stand unmoved, With Christ her
[strength and shield.
all our vast frontier Glad songs shall rise to Jesus, While skeptics turn to hear.

CHORUS.

Re- joice, rejoice, ye workers all, re-joice; O, clap your hands and
Rejoice, rejoice, rejoice,

sing, and sing, O, clap your hands and sing; God's holy church shall triumph yet, triumph yet, triumph yet, And he shall reign our King, shall reign our King.

46 Precious, Loving Saviour.

F. J. C.   J. R. S.

1. Bleeding, dy- ing.—all for me, Precious, loving Saviour; On the cross thy
2. Thou the robe of scorn hast worn, Precious, loving Saviour; Thou reproach hast
3. Thorns have pierced that brow of thine, Precious, loving Saviour; Sinless thou, the
4. Cleanse my poor, unworthy heart, Precious, loving Saviour; Make it pure in

CHORUS.

form I see, Precious, lov- ing Saviour. Bleeding, dying,—all for me,—
meekly borne, Precious, lov- ing Saviour.
guilt was mine, Precious, loving Saviour.
ev - 'ry part, Precious, lov- ing Saviour.

That my soul might dwell with thee, In a blest eternity, Precious, loving Saviour.

49

'Tis so Sweet to Trust in Jesus.

Mrs. Louisa M. R. Stead.   Wm. J. Kirkpatrick.

1. 'Tis so sweet to trust in Je - sus, Just to take him at his word;
2. O, how sweet to trust in Je - sus, Just to trust his cleansing blood;
3. Yes, 'tis sweet to trust in Je - sus, Just from sin and self to cease;
4. I'm so glad I learned to trust thee, Precious Je - sus, Saviour, Friend;

Just to rest up - on his promise; Just to know, "Thus saith the Lord."
Just in sim - ple faith to plunge me 'Neath the healing, cleansing flood.
Just from Je - sus simp - ly tak - ing Life and rest, and joy and peace.
And I know that thou art with me, Wilt be with me to the end.

REFRAIN.

Je - sus, Je - sus, how I trust him! How I've proved him o'er and o'er!

p

Je - sus, Je - sus, precious Je - sus! O for grace to trust him more.

From "Songs of Triumph," by per.

Holding on to Jesus.

Rev. Alfred J. Hough.   T. C. O'Kane.

1. Holding on to Je-sus, with the crown in sight; Holding on to Jesus,
2. If I hold to Je-sus, Jesus holds to me, And each path of du-ty
3. Ere you can unshak-en to the Saviour hold Earth must be forsaken,
4. Bid farewell to pleasure, let the i-dols fall, And the Saviour on-ly

in the dark and light; Tho' the world may tempt me with its luring dross,
plain-ly I can see; O-ver all I tri-umph, and secure-ly stand,
self, and love of gold; Gladly you must suf-fer ev-'ry earthly loss,
be your all in all; Nothing shall disturb you, tho' the tempests toss,

REFRAIN.

Hold-ing on to Je-sus, clinging to the cross. Clinging, clinging,
Hold-ing on to Je-sus by his might-y hand.
Hold-ing on to Je-sus, clinging to the cross.
Hold-ing on to Je-sus, clinging to the cross.

clinging to the cross, Holding on to Je-sus, clinging to the cross.

51

49 Leaning on Jesus alone.

FLORA L. BEST.　　　　　　　　　　　　　　　　　　　JNO. R. SWENEY.

1. A bur-den was laid on my spir - it, Whose weight was too heavy to bear;
2. The shadows of doubt gathered round me, The skies all above me were dim;
3. Then weary I sat by the wayside, The tears falling fast from my eyes,

And so I just leaned upon Je - sus, And his loving heart heeded my prayer.
And scarce could I see thro' the darkness, The road that would lead me to him.
When, lo, on the far - a - way mountains, I beheld the glad morning a - rise.

CHORUS.

Leaning on Jesus, my Refuge and Guide, Leaning on Jesus, what want I beside?

Earth's golden treasures seem nothing but dross,
Since I have anchored my heart to his cross;

Lean - ing, lean - ing, Leaning on Je - sus a - lone.
Leaning, I'm leaning on Je - sus a - lone, Yes, I'm leaning on Je - sus a - lone.

4 Its radiance came down from the hill-tops,
And smiled on the valleys below,
My heart sang aloud in its gladness,
For the beautiful sunshine's bright glow.

5 I looked on face of the Master,
It shone thro' the glory of day;
And, leaning my spirit upon him,
The burden slipped softly away.

From " Gems of Praise," by per.　　52

50 Great Rejoicing.

EDWARD A. BARNES.

JNO. R. SWENEY.

1. There is great re-joicing 'Mid the ho - ly an-gels, When we heed the
2. There is great re-joicing When we look to Je - sus, And whose mercy
3. There is great re-joicing When the Spirit conquers, And the heart has
4. There is great re-joicing When we fol-low Je - sus, And our hope is

Spirit's loving call When we kneel, as sinners, At the feet of Je - sus,
is our on-ly plea; When we come repenting That we long have wandered
let the Saviour in When we ask, be - lieving In the blood that cleanseth,
like a guiding star When, with faith uplifted As we journey homeward,

CHORUS.

Who was made a sac - ri - fice for all.
And ac-cept his pardon full and free. Great re-joic - - ing, great re-
To be washed from all of guilt and sin.
We can almost see the gates a - jar.

joic - ing, When a soul by grace is born a-gain: Great re-joicing in the

presence of the an - gels When a soul by grace is born a - gain.

Let Me Cling to Thee.

FANNY J. CROSBY.

JNO. R. SWENEY.

1. Je-sus, let me cling to thee, Show thy mer-cy now to me;
2. Should I wan-der from thy side, Thou, my ev-er faith-ful guide,
3. Thou wilt hear my soul's complaint, Thou wilt cheer me when I faint,
4. Fold me in thy arms of love, Give me comfort from a-bove;

I am lone-ly, weak, oppressed; I am wea-ry, give me rest.
Wilt re-store me to the right, And in dark-ness grant me light.
Thou hast suf-fered death for me, Je-sus, let me cling to thee.
May thy Spir-it's gen-tle power Save and keep me hour by hour.

CHORUS.

In the healing fount di-vine Cleanse my heart and seal me thine;

Thine for-ev-er would I be,— Je-sus, let me cling to thee.

Linger no Longer.

T. C. O'KANE.

Theme from T. E. PERKINS.

1. Come, need-y sin-ners, Je - sus is wait- ing, Wait- ing to give you
2. Come, come to Je - sus, An - gels are wait- ing, Wait- ing to bear the
3. Come, come to Je - sus, Dear friends are waiting, Wait- ing to greet you
4. Come, come to Je - sus, All things are read - y, Read - y for your re-

peace with - in; Haste to the Sav - iour, Trust in his mer - cy,
news a - bove, Sin - ners are com- ing, Wand- 'rers re - turn- ing,
in their throng; Hap - py in Je - sus, Shar - ing their rap- ture,
turn to - day; Time fast is fleet - ing, Judg- ment is hast'ning,

D. S.—Lin - ger no lon - ger, Come now to Je - sus,

Fine. CHORUS.

Taste all the joys of par - doned sin. Lin - ger no lon - ger,
Seek - ing a - gain a Fa - ther's love.
Sing - ing with them the new, new song.
Come, find sal- va - tion while you may.

Je - sus will save you—save just now.

D. S.

Come now to Je - sus, Low at his foot - stool hum- bly bow; Oh,

53 We are Coming.

FANNY J. CROSBY.   WM. J. KIRKPATRICK.

1. We are coming once again where we oft have met, In the presence of the
2. We are coming, like the sheep that was lost and found On the dark and dreary
3. We are coming to the fount where the life-streams flow, Where the Spirit and the
4. We are coming now by faith, in the morn of youth, We are coming, blesed

Lord our King, Where we gathered at his feet with a bright, bright smile, Where we
mountains cold, We have heard the Shepherd's voice, and we long to dwell In the
Bride say, come; We are waiting at the door at our Father's house, To re-
Lord, to thee; If the shining ones rejoice o'er a new born soul, Oh, how

f REFRAIN.   *mp*   *f*

learned the happy songs we sing.   We are com-ing,   We are
shelt-er of his own dear fold.
ceive his tender welcome home.   We are com-ing,
wonder-ful its worth must be!

mp

coming   To the precious Friend that loves us best; We are coming at his
         We are coming

call, We are coming one and all, In his gen-tle, loving arms to rest.

Wonderful Love of Jesus.

"The love of Christ, which passeth knowledge."
Eph. iii. 19.

E. D. Mund.   E. S. Lorenz.

1. In vain in high and ho-ly lays My soul her grateful voice would raise ; For
2. A joy by day, a peace by night, In storms a calm, in darkness light ; In
3. My hope for pardon when I call, My trust for lift-ing when I fall ; In

who can sing the worthy praise Of the won-derful love of Je - sus?
pain a balm, in weakness might, Is the won-derful love of Je - sus.
life, in death, my all in all, Is the won-derful love of Je-sus

CHORUS.

Won-derful love! won-derful love! Won-der-ful love of Je - sus!

Wonder-ful love! won-derful love! Wonder-ful love of Je - sus!

From "Holy Voices," by per.   57

Lift Up Your Heads.

Mrs. R. N. Turner.   Wm. J. Kirkpatrick.

1. Who is this that cometh strong in might, Strong in glory, great and high?
2. Earth with all its fulness is his own, Made by his almight-y hands!
3. Ho-ly are the plac-es where he dwells: Who shall on his work attend?

O ye ev-erlast-ing doors, ye gates, Lift your heads, he draweth nigh!
All the seas shall praise his holy name, Floods o-bey his high commands!
Who shall dare approach him great in power, And his ho-ly mount as-cend?

It is the Lord, the Lord of hosts, He comes with might this way;
They own his power supreme and great, Rejoic-ing to ful-fill,
Who hath clean hands and undefiled, Who hath pure heart and true,

With ma-jes-ty, and power, and strength He comes, he comes to-day.
In raging storm or heavenly calm, His own al-might-y will.
Let on-ly him draw near the King, And his great glo-ry view.

CHORUS.

Lift up your heads, O ye gates, and be ye lifted up, ye ev-erlasting doors,

And the King of glory shall come in, The King of glory shall come in.

56   **Jesus Loves Thee.**

LAURA MILLER.   JNO. R. SWENEY.

1. Je - sus loves thee, wea - ry soul, Be thou not dis - mayed;
2. Je - sus loves thy pre-cious soul, Be thou not dis - mayed;.
3. Are thine eyes with sor - row dim, Be thou not dis - mayed,
4. From the fount - ain o - pened wide Tar - ry not a - way;

Fine.

He the might - y work has done, He thy ran - som paid.
If thou wilt, he'll make thee whole, He thy ran - som paid.
Je - sus bids thee come to him, He thy ran - som paid.
Plunge beneath its crim - son tide: Je - sus calls to - day.

D. S.—He is wait - ing to for - give; Look, oh, look and live!

CHORUS.   *D. S.*

On - ly on his name believe, Thou a par - don shalt receive;

I Will Follow Jesus.

SALLIE SMITH.   JNO. R. SWENEY.

1. Who is rea-dy? who will say, I have made my choice to-day;
2. What a Saviour! none but he From the law could make us free;
3. Room for all at Je-sus' feet, Room beneath the mer-cy-seat;
4. Hear the lov-ing Spir-it call, Welcome, welcome, one and all;

In the strait and nar-row way I will fol-low Je-sus?
Glad and grate-ful we should be Still to fol-low Je-sus.
Come and taste his love so sweet, Come and fol-low Je-sus.
Ere the eve-ning shadows fall Come and fol-low Je-sus.

CHORUS.

By his grace brave and strong, Ev-er faith-ful, marching on;

In the strait and nar-row way I will fol-low Je-sus.

The Sure Foundation.

T. C. O'KANE.

1. There stands a Rock on shores of time That rears to heav'n its head sublime;
2. That Rock's a cross, its arms outspread, Celes - tial glo - ry bathes its head;
3. That Rock's a tower, whose lofty height, Illumed with heav'n's unclouded light,

That Rock is cleft, and they are blest Who find within this cleft a rest.
To its firm base my all I bring, And to the Cross of A - ges cling.
Opes wide its gate beneath the dome Where saints find rest with Christ at home.

CHORUS.

Some build their hopes on the ev - er drifting sand, Some on their

fame, or their treasure, or their land; Mine's on a Rock that for-

ev - er will stand, Je - sus, the "Rock of A - ges."

59   There's Room for All.

LAURA MILLER.   JNO. R. SWENEY.

1. There's room for all and the feast is spread,—Remember the price it cost;
2. There's room for all at the blood-stain'd cross, There's room by the streams that flow;
3. There's room for all at the door of grace, But why do you still de - lay?
4. There's room for all in our Father's home Prepared by redeeming love;

The Saviour's blood for the world was shed,—Oh, why need a soul be lost?
And, though your sins are of crimson hue, Come, wash them as white as snow.
The light that shines on your pathway now May set ere the close of day.
But on - ly they who are faithful here Can hope for the joys a - bove.

CHORUS.

Room for all, room for all, Come, sinner, come, 'tis the Saviour's call; "Whosoever

will" is roll- ing onward still, "Whosoev - er will may come to Je - sus."

60 In the Shadow of the Rock.

Rev. M. Lowrie Hofford.

Adam Geibel.

1. In the shadow of the rock Let me rest,   O the shade is so re-
2. In the shadow of the rock Let me rest,   When the heat-waves of temp-
3. In the shadow of the rock Let me rest,   When the twilight of the

Let me rest,

fresh- ing, My heart at once is blest; In the weary walk of life, From the
ta - tion Are beating on my breast, When devices of the foe Would al-
evening Is gathering in the west; When the night without a morning On

Fine.

burdens of the day, In the shadow of the rock Let me rest upon my way.
lure my feet astray, In the shadow of the rock Let me rest, and let me pray.
earth is drawing near, In the shadow of the rock Let me rest without a fear.

CHORUS.   D. S.

Let me rest,   Let me rest,   In the shadow of the rock, Let me rest,

Let me rest,   Let me rest,   Let me rest,

61 Rest by and by.

May L. Clayton.   Jno. R. Sweney.

1. I've been to the field with the reapers, And there I have gleaned all day;
2. O sweet was the song of the reapers, And bright was their golden grain.
3. And still by the side of the reapers   I ask that my place may be,

But my task was light, and my heart was glad, For I heard the Master say:
As it waved in the light of the mid-day sun, And it smiled o'er the harvest plain.
Till the sun shall set, and my work is done, And the Master calls me home.

CHORUS.

Rest by and by, rest by and by, Rest in the field a - bove; There is

rest by and by, happy rest by and by, And a crown of e- ter- nal love.

64   DO RE MI FA SO LA SI

Divine Guidance.

MARY D. JAMES.　　　　　　　　　　　　　　　　WM. J. KIRKPATRICK.

1. In this world of sin and dan- ger, How I need a constant guide!
2. While thy mighty hands shall hold me,—Weak and helpless tho' I be,—
3. Trusting in thy loving guid- ance, Peace- ful- ly I tread the way!

Wi - ly foes are all around me, — Je- sus, keep me near thy side.
Safe- ly I shall pass thro' dangers, Fearless of the foes I see.
Looking ev - er un - to Je - sus, Thou wilt never let me stray.

Bless- ed Sav- iour, Blessed Sav - iour, Let me in thy love a - bide;
Dear Redeem - er, Dear Re- deem- er, All my trust is stayed on thee;
Great Pro- tect- or, Great Pro- tect- or, Thou wilt keep me night and day;

Blessed Sav- iour, Blessed Sav- iour, Let me in thy love a - bide.
Dear Redeem- er, Dear Redeem - er, All my trust is stayed on thee.
Great Protect- or, Great Protect- or, Thou wilt keep me night and day.

4 Under thy blest wing of mercy
　How securely do I rest;
Clouds may come, and fearful tempest,
　But I'm leaning on thy breast.
　　Blessed shelter,
　Here no enemies molest.

5 Jesus, how thy loving kindness
　Hedges all my onward path,
How thy mercy doth inclose me!
　"Thou wilt guide me unto death."
　　I will praise thee,
　Praise thee with my latest breath.

　SRJ—2E　　65

Heaven.

T. C. O'KANE.

1. What glo - ry is thine, O thou Ci - ty of God; O Zi - on, bright
2. We know thou hast nev - er a beam of our sun, The moon nor the
3. We dream of thy peace that shall nev - er be strife, The day that shall
4. We see the white robes in the streets of pure gold, The flash of white

land of our dreams, of our dreams, What beauty hangs over thy flower - y sod,
stars of our night; of our night; With grandeur eternal thy arch - es are hung,
nev - er be nev - er be o'er; The lil - ies so white in the Riv - er of Life,
wings in the air; in the air; The star of thy morning that never grows old,

CHORUS.

Thy walls and thy silver-winged streams! To thee we will journey, O
The smile of the Lord is thy light!
The ros - es so sweet on the shore!
The smile of the loved that are there!

Ci - ty of God, To rest on thy evergreen shore, When mortal - ity's

evergreen shore,

pathways of du - ty are trod, With Jesus to live ev - ermore. ev - er - more.

64 In the Book of Life.

LIZZIE EDWARDS. WM. J. KIRKPATRICK.

1. In thy book, where glory bright Shines with never - fad - ing light,
2. In the book, whose pages tell Who have tried to serve thee well,
3. In the book, where thou dost keep Record still of years that sleep,
4. O my Saviour, thou canst show What I long so much to know:

Where thy saved thou wilt re - cord, Write my name, my name, O Lord.
O'er my name let mer - cy trace Child of God, redeemed by grace.
Let my name be writ - ten down Heir to life's im - mor - tal crown.
Let my faith be - hold and see That my life is hid with thee.

CHORUS.

Write my name in the book of life, Lamb of God, write it there;

Where thy saved thou wilt re - cord Write my name, my name, O Lord.

65 Forward, our Watchword.

HENRY ALFORD.   T. C. O'KANE.

1. Forward! be our watchword, Steps and voices joined, Seek the things be-
2. Forward through the desert, Thro' the toil and fight; Jor-dan flows be-
3. Glor - ies upon glor-ies Hath our God prepared, By the souls that
4. Far o'er yon ho-ri-zon Rise the ci-ty towers, Where our God a-

fore us, Not a look be-hind: Burns the fi - ery pil - lar
fore us, Zi - on beams with light! For-ward! flock of Je - sus,
love him One day to be shared: Eye hath not be-held them,
bid - eth That fair home is ours; Forward, marching east-ward

At our army's head; Who shall dream of shrinking, By our Captain led?
Salt of all the earth, Till each yearning purpose Spring to glorious birth:
Ear hath never heard; Nor of these hath uttered Thought or speech a word:
Where the heav'n is bright, Till the veil be lift-ed, Till our faith be sight!

CHORUS.

Forward! forward in the con - flict With the mighty hosts of sin,

The Saviour is our glorious Cap - tain, Sure-ly we shall win.

The Open Arms.

Henrietta E. Blair.   Wm. J. Kirkpatrick.

1. Oh, why are you slighting the Saviour, So patient, forgiv-ing, and true?
2. Once led as a lamb to the slaughter, He suffered, and languished, and died;
3. A-gain the dear Saviour is call-ing, O turn ye, for why will ye die?
4. A-gain the dear Saviour is pleading; Oh, look to his mer-cy and live;

The arms of his mer-cy are o-pen; He of-fers a welcome to you.
And now, in his ten-der compas-sion, He shows you his hands and his side.
Your sun may go down in a moment, The ar-row of death may be nigh.
The pleasures of time are but fleeting, Then trust not the promise they give.

CHORUS

O come to the arms that are wait - ing, They long have been
Come, come, come to the arms that are wait-ing, wait-ing, Come, they long have been

wait-ing for you; Oh, come to your loving Re-
wait - ing for you, wait-ing for you; Come, come, come to your lov - ing Re-

poco rit.

deem - - - er, So gen - tle, forgiving, and true.
deemer, your loving Redeem-er, Gen - tle, gen-tle, for-giv-ing, and true, forgiving and true.

DO RE MI FA SO LA SI

Only a Beam of Sunshine.

FANNY J. CROSBY.　　　　　　　　　　　　　　　JNO. R. SWENEY.

1. On - ly a beam of sun - shine, But oh, it was warm and bright; The
2. On - ly a beam of sun - shine That in - to a dwell - ing crept, Where,
3. On - ly a word for Je - sus! Oh, speak it in his dear name; To

heart of a wea - ry trav - 'ler Was cheered by its wel - come sight.
o - ver a fad - ing rose - bud, A moth - er her vig - il kept.
per - ish - ing souls a - round you The message of love pro - claim.

On - ly a beam of sun - shine That fell from the arch a - bove, And
On - ly a beam of sun - shine That smiled thro' her falling tears, And
Go, like the faith - ful sun - beam, Your mission of joy ful - fil; Re -

ten - der - ly, soft - ly whispered A mes - sage of peace and love.
showed her the bow of prom - ise, For - got - ten perhaps for years.
member the Saviour's prom - ise, That he will be with you still.

CHORUS.

On - ly a word for Je - sus, On - ly a whispered prayer

DO RE MI FA SO LA SI

Only a Beam of Sunshine.—CONCLUDED.

O - ver some grief-worn spir - it May rest like a sun-beam fair.

68   Hail to the Brightness.

THOMAS HASTINGS.   J. J. HOOD.

1. Hail to the brightness of Zi - on's glad morning! Joy to the
2. Hail to the brightness of Zi - on's glad morning! Long by the
3. Lo, in the des - ert rich flow-ers are springing; Streams ov - er
4. See, from all lands, from the isles of the o - cean, Praise to Je -

lands that in dark-ness have lain! Hushed be the ac - cents of
prophets of Is - rael fore - told; Hail to the mil - lions from
co - pious are glid - ing a - long; Loud from the mountain tops
ho - vah as - cend - ing on high; Fallen are the en - gines of

sor - row and mourning; Zi - on in triumph be - gins her mild reign.
bond - age return - ing; Gen - tiles and Jews the blest vision be - hold.
ech - oes are ring - ing; Wastes rise in verdure, and min - gle in song.
war and commotion; Shouts of salva - tion are rend - ing the sky.

Dying, Pleading, Coming.

L. S. N.   JNO. R. SWENEY.

1. Je - sus died on Calvary's mountain, Died for you, died for me;
2. Je - sus rose a - gain vic - torious, Rose for you, rose for me;
3. Je - sus comes a - gain all glorious, Comes for you, comes for me,

From his side a pur - ple fountain Flowed for you, flowed for me.
Now he pleads, our Priest all glorious, Pleads for you, pleads for me.
Bringing crowns for saints vic- torious; One for you, one for me.

We were sin-ners, but he gave us His own precious blood to save us,
Shows his hands and feet all bleeding, What he suffered for us needing
On his Father's throne now seated, All his foes at last de- feat-ed,

Part - ners of his bliss to have us, Je - sus died, Je - sus died.
Ev - er for us in - ter-ced-ing, Je - sus pleads, Je - sus pleads.
By his own redeemed ones greeted, Je - sus comes, Je - sus comes.

Calvary.

" The place which is called Calvary, there they crucified him."

Rev. W. M'K. Darwood.　　　　Luke xxiii. 33.　　　　Jno. R. Sweney.

1. On Calv'ry's brow　　　my Saviour died,　　　'Twas there my
2. 'Mid rending rocks　　　and dark'ning skies,　　　My Saviour
3. O Je-sus, Lord,　　　how can it be,　　　That thou shouldst

Lord　　　was cruci - fied:　　　'Twas on the cross　　　he bled for
bows　　　his head and dies;　　　The opening vail　　　reveals the
give　　　thy life for me,　　　To bear the cross　　　and ag-o-

me,　　　And purchased there　　　my par-don free.
way　　　To heaven's joys　　　and endless day.
ny,—　　　In that dread hour　　　on Cal-va-ry!—

mf CHORUS.　*p*　　　*m*　　　*p*　　　*pp*

O Cal-va-ry! dark Calva-ry! Where Jesus shed his blood for me, for me;

mf　　*ff*　　　*mf*　　　*rit.* *p*

O Cal-va-ry! blest Cal-va-ry! 'Twas there my Saviour died for me.

Seeking for Me.

E. E. HASTY.

1. Jesus, my Saviour, to Bethlehem came, Born in a manger to sorrow and shame;
2. Jesus, my Saviour, on Calvary's tree, Paid the great debt, and my soul he set free;
3. Jesus, my Saviour, the same as of old, While I did wander afar from the fold,
4. Jesus, my Saviour, shall come from on high, Sweet is the promise as weary years fly;

Oh, it was wonder-ful, blest be his name, Seeking for me, for me.
Oh, it was wonder-ful, how could it be? Dy-ing for me, for me.
Gent-ly and long he hath pled with my soul, Calling for me, for ' me.
Oh, I shall see him descending the sky, Coming for me, for me.

for me, ... for me; ....

Seeking for me, seeking for me, Seeking for me, seeking for me
Dy-ing for me, dying for me, Dy-ing for me, dying for me;
Call-ing for me, calling for me, Call-ing for me, calling for me;
Com-ing for me, coming for me, Com-ing for me, coming for me;

Oh, it was wonderful, blest be his name, Seeking for me, for me.
Oh, it was wonderful, how could it be? Dy-ing for me, for me.
Gent-ly and long he hath pled with my soul, Calling for me, for me.
Oh, I shall see him descending the sky, Coming for me, for me.

Tell it Again.

Mrs. M. B. C. Slade.   R. M. McIntosh.

1. In - to the tent where a gyp- sy boy lay, Dy- ing a - lone at the
2. "Did he so love me,—a poor lit - tle boy? Send unto me the good
3. Bending we caught the last words of his breath, Just as he entered the
4. Smiling, he said, as his last sigh he spent, "I am so glad that for

close of the day, News of sal - va - tion we car- ried, said he,
tid - ings of joy? Need I not per - ish? my hand will he hold?
val - ley of death; "God sent his Son!"—"whoso- ev - er?" said he;
me he was sent!" Whispered, while low sank the sun in the west,

REFRAIN.

"No - bo - dy ev - er has told it to me!" Tell it a - gain!
No - bo - dy ev - er the sto - ry has told!"
"Then I am sure that he sent him for me!"
"Lord, I be- lieve, tell it now to the rest!"

Tell it a- gain! Sal- vation's sto- ry repeat o'er and o'er, Till none can

say of the children of men, "No- bo - dy ev - er has told me be- fore."

73 Every Day.

Rev. E. H. Stokes, D. D.   Wm. J. Kirkpatrick.

1. Though there may be shades of sadness Ev'ry day, ev-'ry day, There are
2. You may have your little crosses Ev-'ry day, ev-'ry day; You may
3. Seek to lighten some one's sorrow Ev-'ry day, ev-'ry day; This will
4. Life may have its ho-ly pleasures Ev'ry day, ev-'ry day; And the

golden gleams of gladness Ev'ry day, ev-'ry day; There is joy a-mid the
meet with little loss-es Ev-'ry day, ev'ry day; Never mind! each cross will
bring a sweeter morrow Ev-'ry day, ev-'ry day; Faint, it may be, yet pur-
heart find richest treasures Ev'ry day, ev-'ry day; See, the skies are growing

rit.

sighing, Laughter ringing thro' the crying, Love to love with smiles replying, Ev'ry
lighten, Grief in all your losses brighten, If your hold on God shall tighten Ev'ry
suing, All the christly graces wooing, And some little good be doing, Ev'ry
clearer, Dear ones all becoming dearer, And our home is so much nearer, Ev'ry

CHORUS.

day, ev-'ry day. Ev-'ry day, . . . while on our way   Thro' the

while on our way

world, . . . let come what may,   Going forth with strong desire, To the

let come what may,

rit.

greatest good aspire, From the high, still rising higher, Ev'ry day, ev'ry day.

---

74   **Jesus, I come to Thee.**

FANNY J. CROSBY.   WM. J. KIRKPATRICK.

1. Je - sus, I come to thee, Long-ing for rest; Fold thou thy
2. Je - sus, I come to thee, Hear thou my cry; Save, or I
3. Now let the rolling waves Bend to thy will, Say to the
4. Swift-ly the part-ing clouds Fade from my sight; Yon - der thy

CHORUS.

wea - ry child Safe to thy breast. Rocked on a storm-y sea,
per - ish, Lord, Save or I die.
troubled deep, Peace, peace be still.
bow ap-pears, Love - ly and bright.

Oh, be not far from me. Lord, let me cling to thee, On - ly to thee.

75 Praise ye the Lord.

FANNY J. CROSBY.   WM. J. KIRKPATRICK.

1. Praise ye the Lord, the hope of our sal-va-tion; Praise ye the Lord, our
2. Praise ye the Lord, whose throne is everlasting; Praise ye the Lord, whose

CHO.—Praise ye the Lord, for good it is to praise him; O let the earth his

soul's a-bid-ing trust; Great are his works and wonderful his counsels;
gifts are ev-er new; Praise ye the Lord, whose tender mercy falleth

ma-jest-y proclaim; Shout, shout for joy and bow the knee before him;

Fine.

Praise ye the Lord, the only wise and just. Praise ye the Lord, our strength and our Re-
Pure as the rain and gentle as the dew. Praise ye the Lord, oh, glory! hal-le-

Sing to the harp and magnify his name.

deemer, Praise ye the Lord, his mighty love recall,—Tell how he came from
lujah! Praise ye the Lord, whose kingdom has no end; Praise ye the Lord, who

Chorus. D.C.

bondage to de-liv-er, Tell how he came to purchase life for all.
watcheth o'er the faithful, Praise ye the Lord, our never changing Friend.

76 In the Morning.

LIZZIE EDWARDS.   JNO. R. SWENEY.

1. We are pilgrims looking home, Sad and wea-ry oft we roam, But we
2. O these tender broken ties, How they dim our aching eyes, But like
3. When our fettered souls are free, Far beyond the narrow sea, And we
4. Thro' our pilgrim journey here, Tho' the night is sometimes drear, Let us

know 'twill all be well in the morning; When, our anchor firmly cast, Ev'ry
jewels they will shine in the morning; When our victor palms we bear, And our
hear the Saviour's voice in the morning, When our golden sheaves we bring To the
watch and persevere till the morning; Then our highest tribute raise For the

Fine.

storm-y wave is past, And we gather safe at last in the morn-ing.
robes immor-tal wear, We shall know each other there, in the morn-ing.
feet of Christ our King, What a chorus we shall sing in the morn-ing.
love that crowns our days, And to Jesus give the praise in the morn-ing.

D. S.—sun-ny region bright, When we hail the blessed light of the morn-ing.

CHORUS.

When we all meet a-gain in the morn-ing, On the sweet blooming

D. S.

hills in the morn-ing; Nev-ermore to say good night In that

79

The Master's Call.

FANNY J. CROSBY.

WM. F. SHERWIN. By per.

1. The Mas-ter is come, and call-eth for thee, He stands at the
2. The Mas-ter has come with blessings for thee, A-rise, and his
3. The Mas-ter is come, and call-eth thee now, This moment what
4. He waits for thee still, then haste with de-light, Oh, fly to the

door of thy heart, No friend so for-giv-ing, so gen-tle as he, Oh,
mes-sage re-ceive; Thy ransom is purchased, thy pardon is free, If
joy may be thine; How tender the smile that illum-ines his brow,—A
arms of his love, Press on to that beauti-ful mansion of light, Pre-

REFRAIN.

say, wilt thou let him depart? Patiently wait-ing, earnestly plead-ing,
thou wilt repent and believe.
pledge of his fa-vor di-vine.   Pa-tiently wait - ing, plead - ing,
pared in his kingdom a-bove.

Je-sus, thy Sav-iour, knocks at thy heart, Pa-tient-ly wait-ing,
wait - ing,

ear-nest-ly plead-ing, Je-sus, thy Sav-iour, knocks at thy heart.
plead - - - ing,

78 Praise and Magnify our King.

LIZZIE EDWARDS.   JNO. R. SWENEY.

1. Great is   the Lord, who rul - eth o - ver all! Wake, wake and sing,
2. Great is   the Lord, who spake and it was done; Wake, wake and sing,
3. Great is   the Lord, oh, come with ho - ly mirth; Wake, wake and sing,
4. Great is   the Lord, and ho - ly is his name! Wake, wake and sing.

wake, wake and sing; Down at   his feet   in   ad - o - ra - tion fall,
wake, wake and sing; Hon - or and strength, dominion he has won,
wake, wake and sing, Come and re-joice, ye   na- tions of the earth,
wake, wake and sing; An - gels and men, his wondrous works proclaim,

Praise and mag-ni - fy our King.   O ye redeemed above, Strike, strike your

harps of love, Hail the Blessed One, Hail the Mighty One, Sweetly his

wonders tell, Loud- ly his glo - ry swell, Praise and magni- fy our King.

Copyright, 1882, by JOHN J HOOD.   SRL-2F   81

79 I Hope to Meet You All in Glory.

EMMA PITT.   WM. J. KIRKPATRICK.

1. I hope to meet you all in glo - ry, When the storms of life are o'er;
2. I hope to meet you all in glo - ry, By the tree of life so fair;
3. I hope to meet you all in glo - ry, Round the Saviour's throne above:
4. I hope to meet you all in glo - ry, When my work on earth is o'er;

I hope to tell the dear old sto - ry, On the bles-sed shin-ing shore.
I hope to praise our dear Redeem-er For the grace that brought me there.
I hope to join the ransomed arm - y Singing now redeem-ing love.
I hope to clasp your hands rejoic-ing On the bright e - ter-nal shore.

CHORUS.

On the shin - ing shore, On the gold - en strand, In our
Father's home, In the hap - py land: I hope to meet you there, I
hope to meet you there,—A crown of vict-'ry wear,—In glo - ry.

The Morning Star.

Mrs. S. T. Griswold. T. C. O'Kane.

With spirit.

[are,
1. There's a star that shines on the blest highway, Where the ransom'd heav'n bound
2. The pilgrim, weary and weak in faith, Hath smiled in its beams afar;
3. O narrow and rugged the blood-bought way That leads to the pearly bar,
4. Shall tri-al and sorrow, so sure to come, The peace of the spirit mar?

As a fire by night and a cloud by day—'Tis the Bright and Morning Star.
One died to redeem him,'tis he who saith,"I'm the Bright and Morning Star."
But they who pass it shall walk for aye By the light of the Morning Star.
Nay, brightest in gloom is the light of home,—Of the Bright and Morning Star.

CHORUS.

The Bright and Morning Star, . . the Bright and Morning Star, . . . A

The Bright and Morning Star,   Bright Morning Star,

bea-con light both near and a-far   Is Je-sus, the Morning Star.

From "Jasper and Gold," by per.

81   I am Thine.

Rev. JOHN O. FOSTER, A. M.   JNO. R. SWENEY.

1. I am thine, O Lord, from this moment thine, I have given all to thee,
2. Now my heart is thine, consecrated all, Thro' faith in Christ a - lone,
3. Oh, the joy of soul where the Saviour reigns, In the heart made fully clean,

And this burdened heart is no longer mine, But is thine e - ter - nal - ly.
And I wait the word of thy gentle call That shall make the witness known.
When the guilt has gone and the sinful stains Are no more on th'-spirit seen.

CHORUS.

I am thine,   I am thine,   Through the all - a - ton - ing blood;
I am thine, am thine,   I am thine,

I am thine,   thou art mine, art mine, O thou blessed Son of God.
am thine,

Receive me as I am.

MARIANNE FARMINGHAM.   T. C. O'KANE.

1. "Just as I am," thine own to be, Friend of the young, who lovest me; To

2. In the glad morning of my day, My life to give, my vow to pay, With

3. I would live ev-er in the light, I would work ever for the right, I

con-se-crate my-self to thee, O Je-sus Christ, I come, I come!

no re-serve and no de-lay, With all my heart, I come, I come!

would serve thee with all my might, Therefore to thee I come, I come!

REFRAIN.

I come, O bless-ed Lord, to thee, To thee, the all-a-toning Lamb, Thine

ev-er, on-ly thine to be,—Re-ceive me, Lord, "Just as I am."

4 With many dreams of fame and gold,
Success and joy to make me bold;
But, dearer still, my faith to hold,
For my whole life I come, I come!

5 And for thy sake to win renown,
And then to take my victor's crown,
And at thy feet to cast it down,
O Master, Lord, I come, I come!

83 All with Jesus.

CHARLES H. ELLIOTT.
JNO. R. SWENEY

1. I know not if yon fad-ing sun Will bring the joy of la-bor done,
2. I know not if the morrow's light Shall greet on earth my waking sight,
3. I know not when my Lord will come And take my waiting spirit home,

I know not if my crown is won, But leave it all with Je-sus; In
Or speed my soul to realms more bright, I leave it all with Je-sus; He
But though a stranger here I roam, I leave it all with Je-sus; I

per - fect trust I lean and rest Con-fid-ing on his lov-ing breast; He
guides me with his gracious eye, And grants me hope when others die; In
know not how or when or where My lips may breathe their latest prayer And

knows and gives me what is best,— I leave it all with Je-sus.
bliss or pain he still is nigh,— I leave it all with Je-sus.
bid a-dieu to earth-ly care,— I leave it all with Je-sus.

CHORUS.

All with Je-sus, all with Je-sus, I leave it all with Je-sus; He knows and gives me what is best,— I leave it all with Je - sus.

84
Jesus, My Own.

Priscilla J. Owens.   Wm. J. Kirkpatrick.

1. I wandered in darkness, for - sak - en, a - lone, My hopes were all
2. My heart was so guilt- y, So heav - y with fears, My eyes were all
3. He sooth'd all my sorrow, He pardoned my sin, His touch gave me
4. Sad-heart- ed and weary, Oh, why will you stray, When Je - sus is

withered, And joy was unknown, Till I came to the Saviour, The
blinded With fast flowing tears, When I came to the Saviour, The
healing, His blood made me clean; Now I rest in my Saviour, My
waiting To save you to - day? On- ly look to my Saviour, My

kind, loving Saviour, Till I came to the Saviour, My Je - sus, my own.
kind, loving Saviour, When I came to the Saviour, My Je - sus, my own.
kind, loving Saviour, Now I rest in my Saviour, My Je - sus, my own.
kind, loving Saviour, On- ly look to my Saviour, My Je - sus, my own.

85

Help Just a Little.

As sung by Rev. W. A. Spencer, D. D.

Rev. W. A. Spencer, D. D.   Wm. J. Kirkpatrick.

1. Broth-er for Christ's kingdom sighing, Help a lit-tle, help a lit-tle;
2. Is thy cup made sad by tri-al? Help a lit-tle, help a lit-tle;
3. Though no wealth to thee is giv-en, Help a lit-tle, help a lit-tle;

Help to save the mil-lions dy-ing, Help just a lit-tle.
Sweet-en it with self-de-ni-al, Help just a lit-tle.
Sac-ri-fice is gold in heav-en, Help just a lit-tle.

CHORUS.

Oh, the wrongs that we may righten! Oh, the hearts that we may lighten!

Oh, the skies that we may brighten! Helping just a lit - tle.

4 Let us live for one another,
  Help a little, help a little;
Help to lift each fallen brother,
  Help just a little.

5 Tho' thy life is pressed with sorrow,
  Help a little, help a little;
Bravely look t'ward God's to-morrow,
  Help just a little.

Copyright, 1886, by John J. Hood.

88

Abide with me.

FRANK GOULD.   JNO. R. SWENEY.

1. All the day, ... in sweet commun - ion, . . Je - sus,
2. One by one . . . . . the evening sha - dows . . Gath - er

1. All the day, in sweet commun- ion, All the day, in sweet communion, Je - sus,
2. One by one the evening shadows, One by one the evening shadows Gath - er

I . . . . have walked with thee; . . Do not now . . withdraw thy
dark - - - - ly o'er the lea, ... Yet the light . . of peace re-

I have walked with thee, Jesus, I have walked with thee; Do not now withdraw thy presence, Do not
dark-ly o'er the lea, Gath-er darkly o'er the lea, Yet the light of peace remaineth, Yet the

pres - ence, From this hour . . . . abide with me. . . . .
main - eth . . If thou still . . . . abide with me. . . . .

now withdraw thy presence, From this hour abide with me, From this hour abide with me.
light of peace remaineth If thou still abide with me, If thou still abide with me.

D. S.—ti - tion, Go not hence, . . . abide with me.
prayer, my soul's peti- tion, abide with me, Go not hence, abide with me.

CHORUS.

Thou my life, . . . my on - ly guide, . . . There is naught in heav'n or
Thou my life, my on - ly guide,

D. S.

earth I ask but thee; . . . . Hear my prayer, . . . my soul's pe-
I ask but thee; my soul's peti - tion. Hear my

Anywhere with Thee.

Jennie Garnett.   Jno. R. Sweney.

1. When immor-tal souls are dy - ing, Lord, we would not think of rest;
2. If among the poor and low - ly Thou dost call us by thy grace,
3. Though we may not see the fruit-age Of our toiling here be - low,
4. Choose for us our path of du - ty, Teach us, Lord, our hearts are weak;

But we ask a field of la - bor That will serve and please thee best.
At the post thy will as - signs us We are glad to take our place.
Ev -'ry precious soul we gath - er In the fu-ture we shall know.
May thy blessed, ho - ly Spir - it Give the words that we shall speak.

CHORUS.

Anywhere thy steps to fol - low, On a des-ert though it be;

An - ywhere, if thou but lead us,. An - ywhere, O Lord, with thee.

88 Thy Holy Spirit, Lord, Alone.

Henrietta E. Blair.   Wm. J. Kirkpatrick.

1. Thy Ho - ly Spir - it, Lord, a - lone Can turn our hearts from sin, His
2. Thy Ho - ly Spir - it, Lord, a - lone Can deep- er love in - spire, His
3. Thy Ho - ly Spir - it, Lord, can bring The gifts we seek in prayer, His
4. Thy Ho - ly Spir - it, Lord, can give The grace we need this hour, And

power a - lone can sanc - ti - fy And keep us pure with - in.
power a - lone with - in our souls Can light the sa - cred fire.
voice can words of com- fort speak And still each wave of care.
while we wait, O Spir - it, come In sanc - ti - fy - ing power.

CHORUS.

O Spir - it of Faith and Love, Come in our midst, we pray, And
4th v.—O Spir - it of Love, de- scend, Come in our midst, we pray, And

pur - i - fy each wait- ing heart; Baptize us with pow'r to - day.
like a rush- ing, might- y wind Sweep o - ver our souls to - day.

89 The Coming of His Feet.

Lyman Whitney Allen. Jno. R. Sweney.

1. In the crimson of the morning, in the whiteness of the noon, In the
2. I have heard his weary footsteps on the sands of Gal-i - lee, On the
3. Down the minster isles of splendor, from betwixt the cherubim, Thro' the

am-ber glory of the day's retreat, In the midnight robed in darkness, or the
temple's marble pavement, on the street, With the weight of sorrow falt'ring up the
wond'ring throng, with motion strong and fleet, Sounds his victor tread approaching
[with a

gleaming of the moon, I list - en for the com-ing of his feet.
slopes of Cal-va - ry, The sor-row of the com-ing of his feet.
mu - sic far and dim—The mu - sic of the com-ing of his feet.

CHORUS.

For the com - - - ing of his feet, For the com - -

I am list'ning, I am list-'ning for the com-ing of his feet, I am

- - - ing of his feet; He is coming, hal-le-lu-jah! he is

list'ning for the coming of his feet;

The Coming of His Feet.—CONCLUDED.

com-ing robed in light! I list-en for the com-ing of his feet.

4 Sandaled not with shoon of silver,
 girdled not with woven gold,
Weighted not with shimm'ring gems
 and odors sweet,
White-winged and shod with glory in
 the Tabor-light of old—
The glory of the coming of his feet.

5 He is coming, O my spirit! with his
 everlasting peace,
With his blessedness immortal and
 complete;
He is coming, O my spirit! and his
 coming brings release;
I listen for the coming of his feet.

---

90   Just Beyond.

T. C. O'K.   T. C. O'KANE.

FIRST VOICE.

1. Hear you ev - er   an - gels singing, As   around the throne they shine?
2. Hear you ev - er   in your slumbers Songs from those who've gone before?
3. Do   you ev - er   feel like go - ing To that land   so bright and fair?
4. Let   us cher - ish now and ev - er Glowing hopes   of joys to come,

SECOND VOICE.

Yes, I oft - en hear them chanting, Chanting hymns of love di - vine.
Oh, how oft - en do I hear them, Singing   on   the oth - er shore.
Oh, how oft - en would I glad - ly Go and join   the loved ones there.
And when earthly ties we sev - er Meet in heaven, our hap - py home.

CHORUS.

Heaven's plains are just before   us, Just beyond   the shores of time.

Soon we'll join the mighty cho - rus, In that bright - er, bet - ter clime.

REMARK.—The 1st, 2d, and 3d stanzas should be sung by Solo voices, the 4th stanza as a Duet.

by per.   93

91 "Overcomers."

W. J. K.

QUESTION.

Wm. J. Kirkpatrick.

1 John v. 5, 4. 1. Who, who is he? Who, who is he? Who, who is he that o-ver-
Rev. III. 5. 2. What shall he wear? What shall he wear? What shall he wear that over-
Rev. II. 7. 3. What shall he eat? What shall he eat? What shall he eat that o-ver-
Rev. III. 12. 4. What shall he be? What shall he be? What shall he be that o-ver-

RESPONSE.

com-eth by the blood of the Lamb? He that be-liev-eth and is
com-eth by the blood of the Lamb? He shall be clothed in
com-eth by the blood of the Lamb? He shall eat of the
com-eth by the blood of the Lamb? He shall be a pil-lar in the

born of God, He that be-liev-eth and is born of God,
rai-ment white, He shall be clothed in rai-ment white,
tree of life, He shall eat of the tree of life,
tem-ple of God, He shall be a pil-lar in the temple of God,

He that believeth and is born of God, Shall overcome by the blood.
He shall be clothed in raiment white, That overcomes by the blood.
He shall eat of the tree of life, That overcomes by the blood.
He shall be a pillar in the temple of God, That overcomes by the blood.

O, the precious, precious blood! O, the cleansing, healing flood!

O, the pow'r and the love of God, Thro' the blood of the Lamb!

Rev. iii. 5.

5 ‖: What shall we hear?:‖ that over-
By the blood of the Lamb? [cometh
‖: He shall hear his name con-|fessed in
heaven, :‖
That overcomes by the blood.

Rev. xxi. 7.

6 ‖: What shall he have?:‖ that over-
By the blood of the Lamb? [cometh
‖: God will give him all things, and|
make him his son, :‖
That overcomes by the blood.

Rev. iii. 21.

7 ‖: Where shall he sit?:‖ that over-
By the blood of the Lamb? [cometh
‖: He shall sit with | Jesus, on his
throne, :‖
That overcomes by the blood.

1 John v. 4.

8 ‖: What is the victory?:‖ that over-
By the blood of the Lamb? [cometh
‖: Faith is the victory that | over-
cometh, ‖:
By the blood of the Lamb.

92 All the way long it is Jesus.

1. { O good old way, how sweet thou art! All the way long it is Je - sus;
May none of us from thee de- part; All the way long it is Je - sus. }

CHORUS.

Je - sus, Je - sus, Why, all the way long it is Je - sus.

2 But may our actions always say
We're marching in the good old way.

3 This note above the rest shall swell,
That Jesus doeth all things well.

93

The Saviour with me.

LIZZIE EDWARDS.　　　　　　　　　　　　　JNO. R. SWENEY.

DUET.

1. I must have the Saviour with me, For I dare not walk alone, I must
2. I must have the Saviour with me, For my faith, at best, is weak; He can
3. I must have the Saviour with me In the onward march of life, Thro' the
4. I must have the Saviour with me, And his eye the way must guide, Till I

feel his presence near me, And his arm around me thrown. Then my
whisper words of comfort That no oth - er voice can speak.
tempest and the sunshine, Thro' the bat - tle and the strife.
reach the vale of Jordan, Till I cross the roll- ing tide.

CHORUS.

soul shall fear no ill, Let him lead me where he will,

Then my soul shall fear no ill, fear no ill, Let him lead me where he will, where he will,

I will go without a mur- mur, And his foot-steps follow still.

I will go

96

Walking in the Light.

"Let us walk in the light of the Lord."
Isa. ii. 5.

E. A. BARNES. WM. J. KIRKPATRICK.

1. Liv-ing for the Mas-ter, hap-py in his ser-vice, Do-ing what is
2. Grateful to the Fa-ther for his love and goodness, Keep-ing in the
3. Looking up to Je-sus and in him re-joic-ing, Bear-ing here a

pleasing in his sight; Full of faith and courage, wholly con-se-crat-ed,
paths of peace and right; Patient in your tri-als, gen-tle and forbear-ing,
record pure and bright; Life in him possessing, as a crown in heav-en,

CHORUS.

Brothers, this is walking in the light. Walk - - - ing, blest
Walk-ing in the light,

walk - - - ing! Brothers, are we walking in the light of the Lord;
walk-ing in the light,

Walk - - ing, are we walk - - ing, Walking in the light of the Lord.
Walking in the light, walking in the light,

Copyright, 1886, by JOHN J. HOOD. G 97

95 On the Shoals.

MARY B. REESE.   T. C. O'KANE.

1. A cry comes o-ver the deep, Wailing of dy-ing souls, 'Tis
2. Sweet hope went out with the day, Rudder and com-pass lost; De-
3. Quick! point to the sav - ing Rock Looming from out the deep, Whose

ech-oed in ev - - 'ry heart, "Brothers are on the shoals!" The
spair more dark than the night Crowneth the tem - pest-tossed; No
bea-con the per - iled souls Ev - er will safe - ly keep, No

breakers are dash - ing high, And death is in ev - 'ry wave, And
help may come from the sea, No suc - cor from the land, Say,
matter how fierce the storm,—How madly the bil - low rolls, The

wild - ly ring-eth the cry, "We per - ish with none to save."
must they per-ish, and we Reach nev - er to them a hand?
light of the Guid - ing Star Will bring them off the shoals.

CHORUS. *Vivace.*

Ring out the tide of song, of song, While prayer its burden rolls,

By permission.   98

On the Shoals.—CONCLUDED.

That he who rules the storm, ... Will bring them off the shoals.

96 Salvation is Near.

R. KELSO CARTER.   JAS. WARHURST.

1. Come to Jesus now, and he will give you rest, Lay your doubts and fears aside;
2. Thro' the clouds of sin and trial's darkest gloom, Be of cheer, the day has come;
3. Oh, the Lord has died to ransom ev'ry one, 'Tis salvation full and free;

Fine.

He will take you to his tender, loving breast, Freely now be jus-ti-fied.
There is room for all, in heaven there is room, God will safely bring you home.
We have naught to do, for Jesus all has done, We shall live eter-nal-ly.

D.S.—He will give you perfect love without a fear, And forev-er save your soul.

CHORUS.   D.S.

O, rejoice, the Lord has brought salvation near! Sound his praise from pole to pole;

Copyright, 1887, by JOHN J. HOOD.

In Bethany.

Fanny J. Crosby.   Wm. J. Kirkpatrick.

1. 'Twas good to sit at Je-sus' feet In Beth-a-ny, dear Betha-ny! And
2. His welcome voice with joy they heard In Bethany, dear Bethany! They
3. Whene'er he came their souls were blest In Bethany, dear Bethany! His
4. O Saviour, make these hearts of ours Thy Bethany, dear Bethany! And

feel his ten-der love so sweet, In Beth-a-ny, dear Beth-a-ny!
treasured up each precious word, In Beth-a-ny, dear Beth-a-ny!
presence left a hallowed rest, In Beth-a-ny, dear Beth-a-ny!
grant to us the balmy showers Of Beth-a-ny, dear Beth-a-ny!

CHORUS.

If now our faith and prayers agree, Our grateful hearts as glad may be As

ad lib.

those that Je-sus came to see In Beth-a-ny, dear Beth-a-ny!

At the Cross.

R. Kelso Carter.   Arr. by E. E. Nickerson.

1. O Je-sus, Lord, thy dy-ing love Hath pierced my con-trite heart;
2. A-mid the night of sin and death Thy light hath filled my soul;
3. I kiss thy feet, I clasp thy hand, I touch thy bleed-ing side;
4. My Lord, my light, my strength, my all, I count my gain but loss;

Now take my life, and let me prove How dear to me thou art.
To me thy lov-ing voice now saith, Thy faith hath made thee whole.
O let me here for-ev-er stand, Where thou wast cru-ci-fied.
For-ev-er let thy love enthrall, And keep me at the cross.

CHORUS.

At the cross, at the cross, where I first saw the light, And the

bur-den of my heart roll'd a-way, It was there by

faith I receiv'd my sight, And now I am hap-py night and day!

99

Entire Consecration.

FRANCES RIDLEY HAVERGAL.   Chorus by W. J. K.   WM. J. KIRKPATRICK.

1. Take my life, and let it be Con-se-crat-ed, Lord, to thee;
2. Take my feet, and let them be Swift and beau-ti-ful for thee;
3. Take my lips, and let them be Filled with mes-sag-es for thee;
4. Take my moments and my days, Let them flow in endless praise;

Take my hands and let them move At the impulse of thy love.
Take my voice and let me sing Al-ways, on-ly, for my King.
Take my sil-ver and my gold,— Not a mite would I withhold.
Take my in-tel-lect, and use Ev-'ry power as thou shalt choose.

CHORUS.

{ Wash me in the Saviour's precious blood, the precious blood,
Cleanse me in its pu-ri-fy-ing flood, the healing flood, } Lord, I give to

thee, my life and all, to be, Thine, henceforth, e-ter-nal-ly.

5 Take my will, and make it thine;
It shall be no longer mine;
Take my heart,—it is thine own,—
It shall be thy royal throne.

6 Take my love,—my Lord, I pour
At thy feet its treasure-store!
Take myself, and I will be
Ever, only, all for thee!

By permission.   102

Coming To-day.

FANNY J. CROSBY.   JNO. R. SWENEY.

1. Out on the des-ert, looking, looking, Sinner, 'tis Je-sus looking for thee;
2. Still he is waiting, waiting, waiting, O, what compassion beams in his eye,
3. Lovingly pleading, pleading, pleading, Mercy, tho' slighted, bears with thee yet;
4. Spirits in glory, watching, watching, Long to behold thee safe in the fold;

Tender - ly calling, calling, calling, Hither, thou lost one, O, come unto me.
Hear him repeat-ing gent-ly, gently, Come to thy Saviour, O, why wilt thou die.
Thou canst be happy, hap-py, hap-py, Come ere thy life-star forever shall set.
Angels are waiting, waiting, waiting, When shall thy story with rapture be told?

CHORUS.

Jesus is looking, Jesus is calling, Why dost thou linger, why tarry away?

Run to him quickly, say to him gladly, Lord, I am coming, coming to-day.

101 **We shall Reap by and by.**

MARTHA J. LANKTON.   WM. J. KIRKPATRICK.

1. In the cross of the Sav-iour Our re-joic-ing shall be, In the
2. In the midst of the sha-dows Tho' our seed may be sown, Tho' our
3. Praise the Lord for the prom-ise Of a mansion a-bove, That his
4. Let us work and be joy-ful While the daylight shall last, Let us

cross where he suffered That we all might be free; For the love that came
strength may be weakness, We can trust in his own; He will smile on our
chil-dren may en-ter Thro' his mer-cy and love; When he makes up his
work till the summer And the harvest are past; Then with sheaves ripe and

seek-ing, And has not passed us by, Let us work in his vineyard; Our re-
la-bor Thro' the clouds drifting by, Let us work late and ear-ly; Our re-
jew-els He will not pass us by, Let us work and not wea-ry; Our re-
gold-en Home to rest let us fly, Singing praises to Je-sus With the

CHORUS.

ward is on high. We shall reap by and by, We shall reap by and
4th v. glad ones on high.

by, Let us work and be faith-ful, We shall reap by and by.

Over There.

T. C. O'Kane.

1. O, think of a home over there, By the side of the river of light,
2. O, think of the friends over there, Who before us the journey have trod,
3. My Saviour is now over there, There my kindred and friends are at rest;
4. I'll soon be at home over there, For the end of my journey I see;

Over there,

Where the saints all immortal and fair, Are robed in their garments of white.
Of the songs that they breathe on the air, In their home in the palace of God.
Then away from my sorrow and care, Let me fly to the land of the blest.
Many dear to my heart, over there, Are watching and waiting for me.

Over there.

REFRAIN.

O-ver there, o-ver there, O, think of a home over there,
O-ver there, o-ver there, O, think of the friends over there,
O-ver there, o-ver there, My Saviour is now o-ver there,
O-ver there, o-ver there, I'll soon be at home over there,

Over there, over there, over there,

O-ver there, over there, over there, O, think of a home over there.
O-ver there, over there, over there, O, think of the friends over there.
O-ver there, over there, over there, My Saviour is now over there.
O-ver there, over there, over there, I'll soon be at home over there.

over there,

103 Rejoice, my Soul.

E. A. Barnes.

Jno R. Sweney.

1. In Je - sus, as the on - ly Son, Re - joice, my soul, re - joice;
2. In Je - sus and his words divine Re - joice, my soul, re - joice;
3. In Je - sus, who will help and cheer, Re - joice, my soul, re - joice;
4. In Je - sus, as thy loving Friend, Re - joice, my soul, re - joice;

In Je - sus, as the ho - ly One, Re - joice, my soul, re - joice. In
In Je - sus, who is ev - er thine, Re - joice, my soul, re - joice. He
In Je - sus, who is ev - er near, Re - joice, my soul, re - joice. He
In Je - sus, ev - en to the end, Re - joice, my soul, re - joice. And

that he suffered on the tree, In that he made salva - tion free,
makes thy blessings to increase, Thy faith to soar, thy fears to cease;
loves to bless thy passing days, He loves to keep thee in his ways;
then on life's e - ter - nal shore, Thy pres - ent ills and sorrows o'er,

Fine.

Oh, in the Lord, . . . who purchased thee, Rejoice, my soul, re - joice.
Then in the Lord, . . . who is thy peace, Rejoice, my soul, re - joice.
Then in the Lord, . . . who is thy praise, Rejoice, my soul, re - joice.
Oh, in the Lord, . . . for - ev - er - more, Rejoice, my soul, re - joice.

Rejoice, my Soul.—CONCLUDED.

CHORUS. *D. S.*

Re-joice, my soul, rejoice, Re-joice, my soul, re-joice; . . .

Rejoice, rejoice, my soul, rejoice, my soul, rejoice, Rejoice, rejoice, my soul, rejoice, my soul, rejoice;

104

Our Song of Praise.

T. C. O'KANE.

1. Come, ye that love the Saviour's name, And joy to make it known, The
2. Be- hold your Lord, your Master, crowned With glories all divine; And
3. When in his earthly courts we view The glories of our King, We
4. And shall we long and wish in vain? Lord, teach our songs to rise; Thy

CHORUS.

Sov'reign of your hearts proclaim, And bow before his throne. We come, O
tell the wond'ring nations round How bright those glories shine.
long to love as an - gels do, And wish like them to sing.
love can an - i - mate the strain, And bid it reach the skies. We come,

Lord, to sing thy praise, And fill thy tem- ple now with sacred lays.

O Lord, to sing thy praise,

Ere the Sun goes down.

JOSEPHINE POLLARD. WM. J. KIRKPATRICK.

1. I have work enough to do Ere the sun goes down, For myself and kindred
2. I must speak the loving word Ere the sun goes down; I must let my voice be
3. As I journey on my way, Ere the sun goes down, God's commands I must o-

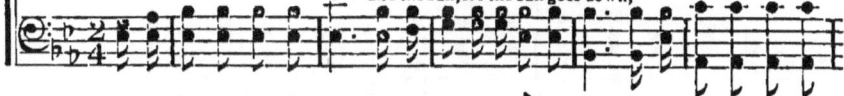

Ere the sun, ere the sun goes down,

too, Ere the sun goes down. Every i-dle whisper stilling, With a
heard Ere the sun goes down; Every cry of pi-ty heeding, For the
bey, Ere the sun goes down. There are sins that need confessing, There are

Ere the sun, ere the sun goes down.

purpose firm and will-ing All my dai-ly tasks ful-fill-ing, Ere the
in-jured in-ter-ced-ing, To the light the lost ones lead-ing, Ere the
wrongs that need redress-ing, If I would ob-tain the bless-ing Ere the

Ere the

CHORUS.

sun goes down. Ere the sun goes down, Ere the sun goes down,
sun, ere the sun goes down. Ere the sun goes down, Ere the sun goes down,

I must do my dai-ly du-ty Ere the sun goes down.

Ere the sun goes down, goes down.

106

Rest.

Rev. E. H. Stokes, D. D.

Jno. R. Sweney.

With feeling.

1. Touch my spir - it with thy Spir - it, Lord of All, my Sav - iour;
2. I have found him, what a treasure!—Found my blessed Sav - iour;
3. I have found him: past my weeping, Blessed, bles - sed Sav - iour;

Let me thy sweet rest in - her - it, This my high - est fa - vor.
This the pleasure of all pleasures, Rest in my dear Sav - iour.
And my soul to thy kind keep- ing I com- mit, dear Sav - iour.

CHORUS.

Rest, sweet rest, rest, sweet rest In my bles - sed Sav - iour;

Rest, sweet rest, rest, sweet rest In my bles - sed Sav - iour.

4 On the earth this heavenly resting
  Comes to me, dear Saviour;
  This is love's own manifesting,
  Through my blessed Saviour.

5 In this rest toil does not weary,—
  Toil for thee, my Saviour;
  In the gloom there's nothing dreary,
  With thee, O my Saviour.

107

W. A. S.

Harvest Time.

Rev. W. A. Spencer, D. D.

1. The seed I have scattered in spring-time with weeping, And watered with
2. An- oth- er may reap what in spring-time I've planted, An- oth - er re-
3. The thorns will have choked, and the summer sun blasted The most of the

tears and with dews from on high; An - oth - er may shout when the
joice in the fruit of my pain,—Not know- ing my tears when in
seed which in spring-time I've sown; But the Lord who has watched while my

har- vesters reaping Shall gather my grain in the "sweet by and by."
summer I faint- ed While toiling sad-heart-ed in sunshine and rain.
wea- ry toil last - ed Will give me a har-vest for what I have done.

CHORUS.

O - ver and o - ver, yes, deep - er and deep- er My heart is pierced

through with life's sor- row- ing cry, But the tears of the sow - er and

Fine.

songs of the reap-er shall min-gle to-geth-er in joy by and by.

D. S.

By and by, by and by, By-and by, by and by, Yes, the

108 **The Blood's Applied.**

R. K. C.

R. KELSO CARTER.

Fine.

1. { The blood's applied! my soul is free, I'm saved, without, with-in;
   { The blood of Je-sus cleanseth me From ev-'ry trace of sin.

D.S.—blood's applied, I'm sanc-ti-fied, It makes me pure with-in.

D. S.

The blood's applied, I'm jus-ti-fied, It par-dons ev-'ry sin; The

2 I've bid farewell to every fear,
   By faith I claim the prize;
   Now I can read my title clear
   To mansions in the skies.

3 Temptations come and trials too,
   While hellish darts are hurled;
   But Jesus saves me through and
   In spite of all the world. [through,

4 Though cares and storms and sorrows
   About me thick and fast, [fall
   My Jesus,—he is Lord of all,—
   Will bring me home at last.

5 Then will my happy, happy soul
   Tell of his love and rest,
   While shouts of victory shall roll
   From every conquering breast.

109

Sing On.

JNO. R. SWENEY.

1. Sing on, ye joy-ful pil-grims, Nor think the moments long;
2. Sing on, ye joy-ful pil-grims, While here on earth we stay
3. Sing on, ye joy-ful pil-grims, The time will not be long

My faith is heav'nward ris-ing With ev-'ry tune-ful song;
Let songs of home and Je-sus Be-guile each fleet-ing day;
Till in our Fa-ther's king-dom We swell a no-bler song,

Lo! on the mount of bless-ing, The glo-rious mount! I stand,
Sing on the grand old sto-ry Of his re-deem-ing love,—
Where those we love are wait-ing To greet us on the shore,

And, look-ing o-ver Jor-dan, I see the promised land.
The ev-er-last-ing cho-rus That fills the realms a-bove.
We'll meet be-yond the riv-er, Where surg-es roll no more.

Copyright, 1885, by Jno. R. Sweney.

112

CHORUS.

Sing on; oh, bliss-ful mu - sic! With ev -'ry note you raise

My heart is filled with rap-ture, My soul is lost in praise:

Sing on; oh, bliss-ful mu - sic! With ev -'ry note you raise

Sing on: bliss - ful, bliss - ful mu - sic,

My heart is filled with rap - ture, My soul is lost in praise.

I've Nothing to Bring.

FLORA L. BEST.   "Wherewith shall I come before the Lord?"—Micah vi. 6.   JNO. R. SWENEY.

Andante.

1. I've noth-ing to bring to thee, Je - sus, But a heart that is
2. I've wandered a - far in the des - ert, Thro' paths that were
3. My Sav-iour, I come at thy bid - ding; I plead by the
4. Oh, joy! like a star a-mong sha-dows, A glim-mer of

sin - ful and sore, And a life that is wea-ry and wast-ed, Yet
thorn-y and wild, The tempests have beaten up - on me, A
thorns on thy brow; By the cross, with its burden of sor-row, Oh,
brightness I see, For One, with a crown on his fore-head, Doth

trembling I knock at the door; I hear the sweet song of the
homeless and sor-row-ful child; But 'mid the be - wil - der - ing
o - pen the door to me now; Perchance, then, when reapers are
o - pen the door un - to me; His arms are out-reached to en-

reap - ers, A - way on the great har-vest plain; I've
maz - es, Thro' clouds that o'er - shadowed the day, There
bear - ing Their sheaves to the har-vest a - bove, I may
fold me; He pil - lows my head on his breast, He

nothing to bring to thee, Je - sus, Not ev - en a sheaf of the grain.
came a sweet voice, and it whispered, "O wander - er, I am the Way."
bring, 'mid the least of the toil - ers, Some blossoms of faith or of love.
bears me from "glory to glo - ry," My soul is e - ter - nal - ly blest.

CHORUS.

Nothing to bring to thee, bring to thee, Still I im - plore, ...
noth - ing to bring, I im - plore,

All my hopes cling to thee, ... O - pen the door,
my hopes cling to thee,

O - pen the door to me, . . . O - - - pen the door. . . .
to me, O - pen, now o - pen the door to me.

115

111 It must be Settled to=night.

A miner in England went to Church one night and became deeply concerned for the salvation of his soul. When the services were ended he refused to leave the house, although the minister told him it was late, and he must go home and seek the Saviour there, and come again the next night. "No," said the miner, "It must be settled to-night, to-morrow night may be too late." So the minister stayed with him until he found peace. The next day while at work in the mines a mass of rock fell upon him, and he was killed. His last words were, "Thank God, it was settled last night, to-night it would have been too late."

Rev. C. B. Kendall.   John J. Hood.

1. "It must be settled to - night, To-morrow may be too late;"
2. A bur - den weighs my soul I can no long - er bear;
3. I can - not rest till peace En - folds me from a - bove,—
4. Oh, now I know 'tis done! My peace is made with God;

The an-gel of death may come, And seal for-ev-er my fate.
Un - less removed this night, 'Twill sink me in - to de - spair.
Till my Redeem - er speaks to me As-sur-ance of his love.
My par-don's found in Je - sus' name, Thro' faith in Je - sus' blood.

CHORUS.

It must be set-tled to - night, I can no long - er wait,
4th v. Oh, now I know 'tis done! Sweet joy pervades my soul;

to-night,

Peace with my God I now must have, To-morrow may be too late.
Peace with my God I now have found; His blood hath made me whole.

112 **He Came to Save Me.**

Henrietta E. Blair.   Wm. J. Kirkpatrick.

1. When Je-sus laid his crown a-side, He came to save me;
2. In my poor heart he deigns to dwell, He came to save me;
3. With gen-tle hand he leads me still, He came to save me;
4. To him my faith with rap-ture clings, He came to save me;

When on the cross he bled and died, He came to save me.
O, praise his name, I know it well, He came to save me.
And trust-ing him I fear no ill, He came to save me.
To him my heart looks up and sings, He came to save me.

CHORUS.

I'm so glad, I'm so glad, I'm so glad that Jesus came, And grace is free,

I'm so glad, I'm so glad, I'm so glad that Jesus came, He came to save me.

113 Sweeping through the Gates.

T. C. O'K. Dying words of Rev. A. Cookman. T. C. O'Kane.

"I'm sweeping through the gates, washed in the blood of the Lamb."

1. Who, who are these be-side the chilly wave, Just on the bor-ders
2. These, these are they who in their youthful days Found Jesus ear-ly
3. These, these are they who in affliction's woes, Ev-er have found in
4. These, these are they who in the conflict dire, Bold-ly have stood a-

of the silent grave, Shouting Je-sus' power to save, Washed in the
and in wisdom's ways, Proved the fulness of his grace, Washed in the
Je-sus calm repose, Such as from a pure heart flows, Washed in the
mid the hottest fire, Jesus now says, "Come up higher;" Washed in the

CHORUS.

blood of the Lamb. "Sweeping thro' the gates" to the New Jerusalem, "Washed
[in the

blood of the Lamb:" "Sweeping thro' the gates" to the New Jerusalem,
in the blood of the Lamb:

"Washed in the blood of the Lamb."

5 Safe, safe upon the ever-shining shore,
Sin, pain, and death, and sorrow all are
Happy now and evermore, [o'er;
Washed in the blood of the Lamb.
Cho.—Sweeping through the streets of, etc.

6 May we, O Lord, be now entirely thine,
Daily from sin be kept by power divine,
Then in heaven the saints we'll join,
Washed in the blood of the Lamb.
Cho.—Sweeping through the streets of, etc.

By permission.   118

Under His Wing.

Edwin H. Nevin, D. D.   Jno. R. Sweney.

1. Un-der his wing I sweetly rest, While balmy peace reigns in my breast;
2. Amidst all dangers seen or known His guardian wing is o'er me thrown;
3. While tossing on the stormy sea, His loving wing still spreads o'er me;
4. The angels with their pinions bright Encamping round me give delight;

I nev-er need a foe to dread, While this bright wing is o'er me spread.
It soothes me with its magic power, And turns to light the darkest hour.
'Mid scenes of conflict and of grief Its presence gives my soul relief.
But with far loftier tone I sing When sheltered 'neath the Saviour's wing.

CHORUS.

Un - - der his wing,   Un - - der his wing,
Un-der his wing,   Un-der his wing, Un-der his wing,   Un-der his wing,

O may my heart for-ev-er sing: Un - - der his wing.
Un-der his wing, shelt'ring wing.

5 His heavenly wing so widely spread
  Is o'er me wheresoe'er I tread;
  It banishes all gloom and fear,
  To feel assured his wing is near.

6 When wasting on the bed of death
  I still can sing with dying breath,
  For round me I can clearly see
  Christ's wing of love o'er-arching me.

The Future.

Miss Jennie Stout.   A. A. Armen.

1. Oh, I oft-en sit and pon-der, When the sun is sink-ing low,
2. Shall I be at work for Je-sus, Whilst he leads me by the hand,
3. But perhaps my work for Je-sus Soon in fu-ture may be done,

Where shall yonder fu-ture find me: Does but God in heav-en know?
And to those a-round be say-ing, Come and join his hap-py band?
All my earthly tri-als end-ed, And my crown in heav-en won;

Shall I be a-mong the liv-ing? Shall I min-gle with the free?
Come, for all things now are rea-dy, Come, his faithful foll-'wer be;
Then for-ev-er with the ran-somed Thro' e-ter-ni-ty I'd be

Where-so-e'er my path be lead-ing, Saviour, keep my heart with thee.
Oh, where'er my path be lead-ing, Saviour, keep my heart with thee.
Chanting hymns to him who bought me With his blood shed on the tree.

CHORUS.

Oh, the fu - - - - ture lies be-fore   me, And I
Oh, the fu-ture lies be-fore me, And I know not where I'll be,   Oh, the

The Future.—CONCLUDED.

know . . not where I'll be,   But where'er - - my path be
future lies before me, And I know not where I'll be, But where'er my path be leading, Saviour,

lead - - ing, Saviour, keep . . . my heart with thee.
keep my heart with thee, But where'er my path be leading, Saviour, keep my heart with thee.

116 Then, oh! then.

EDW. A. BARNES.   WM. J. KIRKPATRICK.

1. The day will soon be past; The light is fading fast; The call will come at last;
2. The voyage will soon be o'er; The billows rage no more; 'Tis near the peaceful shore;
3. The sands are running low; The tide will cease to flow; The final trump will blow;
4. The goal will soon be won; The race will soon be run; 'Tis near the set of sun;

REFRAIN.

And then, oh! then: Then, a perfect day;   Then, a blessed
perfect day;

home;   Then, a golden crown and harp In the world to come.
bles-sed home;

117 ᵺcar ᵹy Call.

FANNY J. CROSBY.   CHAS. J. TAYLOR.

Animated.

1. Light of all who come to thee, Let me now thy glo-ry see, Shining
2. Hope of all who trust in thee, Thou whose blood was shed for me, Thro' its
3. In thy strength, and not my own, This I ask before thy throne, Blessed
4. When on earth I close mine eyes, When to life thou bidst me rise, To thy-

CHORUS.

down with beams divine, Mak-ing glad this heart of mine.   Hear my
heal - ing power divine Keep from sin this heart of mine.
Lord, my faith increase, Keep my soul in   per - fect peace.
self, thou Friend divine, Take, oh, take this heart of mine.

call,   oh, hear my call, Thou my life,   my all in all;   By thy
Hear my call, oh, hear my call,   Thou my life,   my   all in all;

hand   uphold me still,   With thy love   my spir-it fill.
By thy hand   up - hold me still, With thy love my long - ing spir - it fill.

118

To the Rescue.

LIZZIE EDWARDS.
JNO. R. SWENEY.

1. As we journey by the wayside, Rushing onward, to and fro, Oh, the
2. They are thirsting for the water, That their souls may drink and live; They are
3. Once He journeyed by the wayside,—Praise and glory to his name!—Richest

many we may rescue From the path of sin and woe; Sad and lonely, heavy-
longing for the comfort That a better life will give; Hear the pleading voice of
blessing, sweetest comfort, Filled the soul where'er he came; And the poorest of his

ad lib. *a tempo.*

hearted, None to heed their plaintive cry, Can we leave them thus to perish?
mer - cy, Bending now her loving eye, Jesus will not leave them friendless,
creatures That to him for refuge fly, Tho' a heartless world forsake them,

CHORUS.

Can we pass them coldly by. Save them now! save them now! Christian worker,
He will never pass them by.
He will never pass them by.

ad lib.

where art thou? To the rescue hasten quickly, Je- sus calleth, Save them now!

F   123

119 We are More than Conquerors.

"Stand ye still, and see the salvation of the Lord."
2 Chron. xx. 17.

Mrs. Flora D. Harris.　　　　　　　　　　　　　　　　Jno. R. Sweney.

1. What shall separate us From the love that bought us? Shall the pangs of anguish
2. Things to come or present, Whatso'er betide us,—Life nor death shall ever
3. Depths that are beneath us, Heights that are above us, Have no power to sunder,

Which the cross hath wrought us? Doubtings and distresses, Fier-y tri-als
From our Lord divide us; Angels, powers, do-min-ions, These shall fall be-
Since he stooped to love us. Prince of our Redemp-tion, Sons to glo-ry

prove us; Yet am I per-suad-ed, None of these shall move us.
fore us; Clothed in his sal-va-tion, With his banner o'er us.
bring-ing, Thou hast made from sin-ners Victors, crowned and singing.

CHORUS.

We are more than conquerors, More, yea, more; We are more than conquerors,
More, yea, more, more, yea, more;

More, yea, more; We are more than conquerors, We are more than
More, yea, more, more, yea, more;

We are More, etc.—CONCLUDED.

conquer-ors, We are more than conquerors Thro' him that loved us.

120 More Faith in Jesus.

HENRIETTA E. BLAIR.   WM. J. KIRKPATRICK.

1. While struggling thro' this vale of tears I want more faith in Je-sus; A-
2. To war against the foes with-in I want more faith in Je-sus; To
3. To brave the storms that here I meet I want more faith in Je-sus; To
4. I want a faith that works by love, A constant faith in Je-sus; A

D. S.—And

Fine. CHORUS.

mid tempta-tions, cares, and fears, I want more faith in Je - sus. I
rise a-bove the powers of sin I want more faith in Je - sus.
rest con-fid-ing at his feet I want more faith in Je - sus.
faith that mountains can remove, A liv-ing faith in Je - sus.

this my cry, as time rolls by, I want more faith in Je - sus.

D.S.

want more faith, I want more faith, A clearer, brighter, stronger faith in Jesus;

Copyright, 1885, by JOHN J. HOOD.   125

121 Able and Willing to Save.

Rev. E. A. Hoffman.　　　　　　　　　　　　　　　　　　　T C O'Kane.

1. We praise thee, O God, for the Son of thy love, For Je-sus who
2. The moment a sin-ner on Je-sus believes, That moment a
3. O, wondrous redemption, the purchase of blood, Secured thro' the
4. Re-ceive then, my brother, the mes-sage of God, And plunge thyself

died and is now gone a-bove, Him-self for our ran-som he
par-don for sin he re-ceives; And no one in vain his for-
death of the dear Son of God! His life as a ran-som for
in-to the fount-ain of blood; And thou an e-ter-nal de-

wil-ling-ly gave, And he is a-bundant-ly a-ble to save.
giveness shall crave, Since he is so read-y and wil-ling to save.
sin-ners he gave, And now he stands read-y to par-don and save.
liv'rance shalt have, For Je-sus is read-y to par-don and save.

CHORUS.

The sin - - ner to save . . . his life - blood he gave; . . .
The sinner to save, the sinner to save, his life-blood he gave, his life-blood he gave;

He's a - - ble and wil - - ling to par-don and save.
He's a-ble and willing, he's a-ble and willing to pardon, yes, pardon and save.

126

122

Let Him In.

Rev. J. B. ATCHINSON.　　　　　　　　　　　　　　　　E. O. EXCELL.

1. There's a stranger at the door,　Let him in,
2. O-pen now to him your heart,　Let him in,
3. Hear you now his lev-ing voice?　Let him in,
4. Now admit the heavenly Guest,　Let him in,

Let the Saviour in,　let the Saviour in,

He has been there oft be - fore,　Let him in;
If you wait he will de - part,　Let him in;
Now, oh, now make him your choice,　Let him in,
He will make for you a feast,　Let him in,

Let the Saviour in,　let the Saviour in,

Let him in ere he is gone,　Let him in the Ho - ly One,
Let him in, he is your Friend,　He your soul will sure de - fend,
He is stand-ing at the door,　Joy to you he will re - store,
He will speak your sins for-given,　And when earth ties all are riven,

Je-sus Christ, the Father's Son,　Let him in.
He will keep you to the end,　Let him in.
And his name you will a - dore,　Let him in.
He will take you home to heaven,　Let him in.

Let the Saviour in.　let the Saviour in.

Jesus is Passing this Way.

E. A. H.   J. H. Tenney.

1. Is there a sin-ner a-wait-ing Mer-cy and pardon to-day?
2. Brother, the Master is wait-ing, Waiting to free-ly for-give;
3. Yes, he is coming to bless you, While in con-trition you bow;

Welcome the news that we bring him: "Je-sus is passing this way!"
Why not this moment accept him, Trust in his grace, and live?
Coming from sin to re-deem you, Read-y to save you now;

Coming in love and in mer - cy, Pardon and peace to be - stow.
He is so ten-der and pre-cious, He is so near you to-day;
Can you re-fuse the sal - va - tion Je-sus is of-fer-ing here?

Coming to save the poor sin - ner From his heart-anguish and woe.
Open your heart to re-ceive him While he is passing this way.
Open your heart to ad-mit him While he is coming so near.

CHORUS.

Je-sus is passing this way . . . To-day, . . , to-day! . . .
Je-sus is passing this way, To-day, is passing to-day!

Jesus is Passing.—CONCLUDED.

While he is near, oh, believe him, Open your heart to receive him, For

Je-sus is passing this way,... Is passing this way to - day.

this way,

124

Hallelujah.

Wm. G. Collins.

Wm. J. Kirkpatrick.

1. I am glad, oh, so glad, That to Je-sus I came, He has pardoned my
2. Oh, the fullness of joy My Redeem-er to know, And to feel that his
3. Perfect peace in my heart Jesus now gives to me, From all fearing and
4. Saviour, keep me, I pray, Ev - er keep me thine own, Till I join the glad

CHORUS.

sins, I can now praise his name. Halle- lu-jah, Jesus saves me With a
blood Makes me whiter than snow.
doubt- ing, My spir - it is free.
song Of the blest 'round thy throne.

per- fect sal- vation, Hallelu- jah, halle - lu- jah, Jesus saves me just now.

125 Make me a Worker for Jesus.

Eden E. Rexford.   "And every man to his work."—Mark xiii. 34.   T. C. O'Kane.

1. Make me a work-er for Je - sus, Steadfast and earnest and true;
2. Let me be brave in the con - flict, Read- y to go where he needs,
3. Let me go out to the har - vest, Faithful- ly doing my part,
4. Make me a work- er for Je - sus, Trusting him nev- er in vain,

Willing to work for the Mas - ter, What he would have me to do.
Sowing good seed for the har - vest, Plucking up bri- ars and weeds.
Gathering sheaves for the glean- ing, Steadfast of purpose and heart.
Glad if I bind for the Mas - ter Sheaves of God's beautiful grain.

CHORUS.

Make me a worker for Je - sus, Humble my la- bor may be, But

cheer- ful- ly done for the Mas- ter, Who hath done great things for me.

126

The Healing Touch.

"When she heard of Jesus, came in the press behind, and touched his garment."
Mark v. 27.

Mrs. E. C. ELLSWORTH.

WM. J. KIRKPATRICK.

1. An ea - ger, restless crowd drew near, And round the Saviour pressed;
2. The mul - ti-tude, with curious eyes, Just gazed up-on his face;
3. Oh, near to Christ the man - y came, In that most fa - vored hour!
4. Of all who throng his courts to-day Who shall re - ceive his word?

But one, with warm and lov-ing faith, His heal-ing power confessed.
But she glanced up with hope and love, To feel his sav - ing grace.
But one stretched out the hand of faith, And touched his healing power.
Who shall reach forth with faith sincere To touch the heal-ing Lord?

CHORUS.

She had touched the hem of his garment, Trusting with all her soul;
last v. Come and touch the hem of his garment, Trusting with all your soul;

For ev - 'ry touch of the lov-ing Je-sus Can make the wounded whole.

Steer Straight for Me.

T. C. O'KANE.

1. I remember a voice which once guided my way, When tossed on the sea, fog-en-
2. I remember that voice, as it led our lone way 'Mid rocks and thro' breakers and
3. That voice is now hush'd which once guided my way, The form I then press'd is now
4.   I remember that voice in the oft lonely hour, It comes to my heart with fresh

shrouded   I   lay: 'Twas the voice of a child as he stood on the shore, It
high dashing spray; Oh, how sweet to my heart did it sound from the shore As it
mingling with clay; But the tones of my child still resound in my ear, The
beau- ty and power, And still echoes far out over life's troubled wave, And

sound- ed like music o'er the dark billows' roar: "Come this way, my father!
ech- oed so clear- ly o'er the dark billows' roar: "Come this way, my father!
voice of my darling how distinct- ly I hear: "I'm calling you, fa- ther!
sounds from the loved lips that lie in the grave: "Come this way, my father!

REFRAIN.
Softly.

steer straight for me, Here safe on the shore I am waiting for thee." "Come this way, my
steer straight for me, Here safe on the shore I am waiting for thee."
   tossed on life's sea, And on a bright shore I am waiting for thee."
steer straight for me, Here safely in heav'n I am waiting for thee."

Steer Straight for Me.—CONCLUDED.

rit.

father! oh, steer straight for me, Here safe on the shore I am waiting for thee."

128 Nearer.

ANON

T. C. O'KANE.

1. When sunbeams gild my way, Se - rene the sky, Tempt - ing my
2. When tempests shroud the day, And earth is drear, Be thou, O
3. When life's last puls- es wane, Je - sus, be near, My sink-ing

soul to stray By earthly joy: Lord, may thy gifts then be
God, my stay; My sadness cheer, And through the gath'ring night,
heart sus-tain; Ban - ish my fear. To thee my hands shall cling;

Fingers that point to thee, Glad voices calling me Near-er to thee.
Lead upward to the light, Thro' portals ev-er bright· Near-er to thee.
Of thee my lips shall sing; My soul in glo-ry bring, Near-er to thee.

Copyright, 1886, by T C O'Kane.

133

1. Cast thy bread up-on the wa-ters, Ye who have but scant supply,
2. Cast thy bread up-on the wa-ters, Poor and weary, worn with care,—
3. Cast thy bread up-on the wa-ters, Ye who have a-bundant store;
4. Cast thy bread up-on the wa-ters, Far and wide your treasures strew,
5. Cast thy bread up-on the wa-ters, Waft it on with praying breath,

An - gel eyes will watch above it;— You shall find it by and by!
Oft - en sitting in the shadow, Have you not a crumb to spare?
It may float on man-y-a bil-low, It may strand on many-a shore;
Scat - ter it with willing fin-gers, Shout for joy to see it go!
In some distant, doubtful moment It may save a soul from death;

He who in his righteous balance Doth each human ac-tion weigh
Can you not to those around you Sing some lit-tle song of hope,
You may think it lost for-ev - er, But, as sure as God is true,
For if you do close-ly keep it, It will on-ly drag you down;
When you sleep in solemn silence, 'Neath the morn and evening dew,

Will your sac - ri - fice remem-ber, Will your loving deeds re-pay.
As you look with longing vision Thro' faith's mighty tel - e-scope?
In this life or in the oth - er, It will yet return to you.
If you love it more than Je-sus, It will keep you from your crown,
Stranger hands, which you have strengthened, May strew lilies over you.

Meet me There.

Henrietta E. Blair.   Wm. J. Kirkpatrick.

1. On the happy, golden shore, Where the faithful part no more, When the
2. Here our fondest hopes are vain, Dearest links are rent in twain; But in
3. Where the harps of angels ring, And the blest for-ev - er sing, In the

storms of life are o'er, Meet me there; Where the night dissolves away Into
heav'n no throb of pain, Meet me there; By the river sparkling bright, In the
palace of the King, Meet me there; Where in sweet communion blend Heart with

Fine.

pure and perfect day, I am going home to stay, Meet me there.
ci - ty of delight, Where our faith is lost in sight, Meet me there.
heart, and friend with friend, In a world that ne'er shall end, Meet me there.

D.S.—happy golden shore, Where the faithful part no more, Meet me there.

CHORUS.

Meet me there,   Meet me there,   Where the tree of life is

D.S.

blooming, Meet me there;   When the storms of life are o'er, On the

Meet me there;

131 By the Grace of God we'll Meet.

FANNY J. CROSBY. JNO. R. SWENEY.

1. Thro' the gates of pearl and jasper To the ci-ty paved with gold, When the
2. When the harvest work is ended, And the summer days are past, When the
3. Let us fol-low on with firmness, keeping ev-er in the way Where our

ransomed host shall en-ter, And their gracious Lord be-hold, When they
reap-ers go re-joic-ing To their bright re-ward at last; When the
bles-sed Lord has taught us, To be faith-ful, watch and pray; Then, in

meet in bliss-ful triumph By the tree of life so fair Shall we
white-robed an-gel leads them to the gates of joy so fair, Shall we
garments pure and spotless, By the tree of life so fair, We shall

join the no-ble arm-y, And re-ceive a wel-come there?
join their hap-py num-ber? Will they bid us wel-come there?
sing through endless ag-es With the count-less mil-lions there.

CHORUS.

By the grace . . . . . of God we'll meet . . . . . In the
By the grace of God we'll meet, By the grace of God we'll meet In the

ci - - ty's golden street,   Shouting, glo - - - - - ry ! hal-le-
ci - ty's gold - en   street, golden street, Shouting, glo- ry ! hal- le- lu - jah ! Shouting,

lu - - - - jah !   At the dear - - - - - Redeem-er's feet.
glo - ry ! hal - le - lu - jah ! At   our   dear   Re-deem-er's feet,   Re-deem-er's feet.

132   Jesus Lives Forever.

Rev. JAMES MORROW. D. D.   WM. J. KIRKPATRICK.

1. Sing, ye people, loud and high, Jesus lives forever! He is Lord of earth and sky,
2. Come, ye people, here is rest—Jesus lives forever; As the birds return to nest,
3. Pray, ye people, night and day, Jesus lives forever; Mountains, nations may decay,
4. Hope, ye people, fear no doom, Jesus lives forever; Sunlight glints o'er pain and gloom,

To his people ever nigh; We must suffer, we must die, But Jesus lives forever.
Souls find answer to their quest Leaning on his welcome breast, Our Jesus lives forever.
Golden thrones become as clay, Art and science pass away, But Jesus lives forever.
Faith will triumph, tho' we soon touch the shadows of the tomb, For Jesus lives forever.

133 Cast thy Burden on the Lord.

"Casting all your care upon him, for he careth for you."

W. J. K.   1 Pe. v. 7.   WM. J. KIRKPATRICK.

1. Weary pil - grim on life's pathway, Struggling on beneath thy load,
2. Are thy tir - ed feet unstead - y? Does thy lamp no light af- ford?
3. Are the ties of friendship severed? Hushed the voices fondly heard?

Hear these words of con - sol - a - tion,—"Cast thy burden on the Lord."
Is thy cross too great and heav - y? Cast thy bur - den on the Lord.
Breaks thy heart with weight of anguish, Cast thy bur - den on the Lord.

CHORUS.

Cast thy burden on the Lord, Cast thy burden on the Lord, And he will

strengthen thee, sustain and comfort thee; Cast thy bur - den on the Lord.

4 Does thy heart with faintness falter?
  Does thy mind forget his word?
Does thy strength succumb to weakness?
  Cast thy burden on the Lord.

5 He will hold thee up from falling,
  He will guide thy steps aright;
He will strengthen each endeavor;
  He will keep thee by his might.

Treasures of Heaven.

T. C. O'K.

T. C. O'KANE.

1. There's a crown in heaven for the striving soul, Which the blessed Jesus him-
2. There's a joy in heaven for the mourning soul, Tho' the tears may fall all the
3. There's a home in heaven for the faithful soul, In the man-y mansions pre-

self will place On the head of each who shall faithful prove, Ev-en
earth-ly night; Yet the clouds of sadness will break a-way, And re-
pared a-bove, Where the glo-ri-fied shall for-ev-er sing, Of a

REFRAIN.

un-to death, in the heavenly race. O may that crown . . . in heav'n be
joicicing come with the morning light. O may that joy . . . . in heav'n be
Saviour's free and unbound-ed love. O may that home . . . in heav'n be

mine, And I a-mong . . . . the angels shine; Be thou, O
in heav'n be mine, And I among the angels shine;

Lord, ... my daily guide, Let me ev-er in thy love a-bide.
Be thou, O Lord, my daily guide,

135 Ah! 'tis the Old, Old Story.

Mrs. C. L. Shacklock.　　　　　　　　　　　　　　Wm. J. Kirkpatrick.

1. Ah! 'tis the old, old sto - ry, Tempted and led a - stray,
2. Robbing the heart of lightness, Losing the bloom of youth,
3. But, in an old, old sto - ry, Full of a grace di - vine,

Leaving the path of du - ty, Choosing the e - vil way,
Dimming the eyes' glad brightness, Stilling the voice of truth,
There is a-bun-dant par - don, Ev - en for sin like thine,

Breaking the hearts of mothers, Slighting their fervent prayers,
Missing the pride of man - hood, Missing a no - ble aim,
Now, with a contrite spir - it, Turn from the ways of sin,

Sowing the seed which bringeth On - ly a wealth of tares.
Gaining a ship-wrecked na-ture, Gaining a sul - lied name.
Knock at the gate of heav - en, Entrance thy soul shall win.

CHORUS.

Ah! 'tis the old, old sto - ry, Ah! 'tis the old, old sto - ry,
Last cho.—Yes, 'tis the old, old sto - ry, Yes, 'tis the old, old sto - ry,

140

Ah! 'tis the Old, Old Story.—CONCLUDED.

Ah! 'tis the old, old sto - ry, Tempted and led a - stray.
Yes, 'tis the old, old sto - ry, Full of a grace di - vine.

136 I'm With Thee Every Hour.

Mrs. R.

JNO. R. SWENEY.

1. I'm with thee every hour, My word is ever sure; I'll cleanse thee by my
2. I'm with thee every hour, I am the living bread; If thou but test its
3. I'm with thee every hour, I living waters give; Flee then, to faith's strong
4. I'm with thee every hour, My flesh is meat indeed; My blood's all cleansing
5. I'm with thee every hour, Thou weary, laden, come! A mansion is thy

CHORUS.

power, And keep thee always pure. I'm with thee, O, I'm with thee! Thy
power, Thou art for - ev - er fed.
tower, Stoop, thou, and drink and live.
power Is suit - ed to all need.
dower, My Father's house is home.

nev - er failing friend; Lo! I am with thee always, Unto the end.

Saw Ye My Saviour.

SCOTCH MELODY.

1. Saw ye my Sav - iour, saw ye my Sav - iour, Saw ye my
2. He was ex - tend - ed, he was ex - tend - ed, Shame - ful - ly
3. Je - sus hung bleed-ing! Je - sus hung bleed - ing! Three dreadful
4. Darkness pre - vail - ed! dark-ness pre - vail - ed! Darkness pre-

Sav - iour and God? Oh! he died on Cal - va - ry To a-
nailed to the cross; Oh! he bowed his head and died; Thus my
hours in pain; Oh! the sun re-fused to shine When his
vailed o'er the land; Oh! the sol - id rocks were rent, Thro' cre-

tone for you and me, And to pur - chase our par - don with blood.
Lord was cru - ci - fied To a - tone for a world that was lost.
ma - jes - ty di - vine Was de - rid - ed, in - sult - ed, and slain.
a - tion's vast ex - tent, When the Jews cru - ci - fied the God-man.

5 When it was finished, when it was fin-
And the atonement was made, [ished,
He was taken by the great,
And embalmed in spices sweet,
And was in a new sepulchre laid.

6 Hail, mighty Saviour! hail, mighty
Saviour!
Prince, and the Author of peace!
Oh, he burst the bands of death,
And, triumphant from the earth,
He ascended to mansions of bliss.

7 Now interceding, now interceding,
Pleading that sinners may live;
Crying, "Father, I have died;
(Oh, behold my hands and side!)
To redeem them—I pray thee, forgive!"

8 "I will forgive them, I will forgive
them,
If they repent and believe;
Let them now return to thee,
And be reconciled to me,
And salvation they all shall receive."

How do Thy Mercies.

C. Wesley.

Tune, FEDERAL STREET. L. M.

1. How do thy mercies close me round! Forev-er be thy name a-dored;
2. Inured to pov-er-ty and pain, A suff'ring life my Mas-ter led;

I blush in all things to a-bound; The servant is a-bove his Lord.
The Son of God, the Son of Man, He had not where to lay his head.

3 But lo! a place he hath prepared
  For me, whom watchful angels keep;
Yea, he himself becomes my guard;
  He smooths my bed, and gives me sleep.

4 Jesus protects; my fears, be gone;
  What can the Rock of Ages move?
Safe in thy arms I lay me down,
  Thine everlasting arms of love.

5 While thou art intimately nigh,
  Who, who shall violate my rest?
Sin, earth, and hell I now defy:
  I lean upon my Saviour's breast.

6 I rest beneath the Almighty's shade;
  My griefs expire, my troubles cease;
Thou, Lord, on whom my soul is stayed,
  Wilt keep me still in perfect peace.

139 C. Wesley. Depth of Mercy!

Tune, PLEYEL'S HYMN. 7s.

1. Depth of mer-cy! can there be Mer-cy still reserved for me?

Can my God his wrath for-bear,— Me, the chief of sin-ners, spare?

2 I have long withstood his grace;
  Long provoked him to his face;
Would not hearken to his calls;
  Grieved him by a thousand falls.

3 Now incline me to repent;
  Let me now my sins lament;
Now my foul revolt deplore,
  Weep, believe, and sin no more.

4 Kindled his relentings are;
  Me he now delights to spare;
Cries, "How shall I give thee up?"
  Lets the lifted thunder drop.

5 There for me the Saviour stands,
  Shows his wounds and spreads his
God is love! I know, I feel; [hands,
  Jesus weeps, and loves me still.

140 The Stranger at the Door.

Rev. iii. 20.

T. C. O'KANE.

1. Behold a stranger at the door, He gently knocks—has knocked before,
2. O love-ly at-titude,—he stands With melting heart and open hands;
3. But will he prove a friend indeed? He will,—the very friend you need;

Has wait-ed long, is wait-ing still; You treat no oth-er friend so ill.
O matchless kindness, and he shows This matchless kindness to his foes.
The friend of sin-ners? Yes, 'tis he, With garments dyed on Cal-va-ry.

CHORUS.

Oh, let the dear Saviour come in, He'll cleanse the heart from sin ; Oh,

come in,

from sin;

keep him no more out at the door, But let the dear Saviour come in. come in.

4 Rise, touched with gratitude divine,
Turn out his enemy and thine;
That soul-destroying monster, Sin,
And let the heavenly Stranger in.

5 Admit him, ere his anger burn,—
His feet, departed, ne'er return;
Admit him, or the hour's at hand
You'll at His door rejected stand.

Lo! Round the Throne.

MARY L. DUNCAN.   Tune, PARK STREET. L. M.

1. Lo! round the throne, a glo-rious band, The saints in count-less myr-iads stand; Of ev-'ry tongue redeemed to God, Arrayed in garments washed in blood, Arrayed in garments washed in blood.

2 Through tribulation great they came;
They bore the cross, despised the shame;
But now from all their labors rest,
In God's eternal glory blest.

3 They see the Saviour face to face;
They sing the triumph of his grace;
And day and night, with ceaseless praise,
To him their loud hosannas raise.

4 O may we tread the sacred road
That holy saints and martyrs trod;
Wage to the end the glorious strife,
And win, like them, a crown of life!

142   Now to the Lord.

1 Now to the Lord a noble song:
Awake, my soul, awake, my tongue;
Hosanna to the eternal name,
And all his boundless love proclaim.

2 See where it shines in Jesus' face,
The brightest image of his grace;
God, in the person of his Son,
Has all his mightiest works outdone.

3 The spacious earth and spreading flood
Proclaim the wise and powerful God;

And thy rich glories from afar
Sparkle in every rolling star.

4 Grace! 'tis a sweet, a charming theme,
My thoughts rejoice at Jesus' name;
Ye angels, dwell upon the sound,
Ye heavens, reflect it to the ground.

5 Oh! may I reach that happy place,
Where he unveils his lovely face,
Where all his beauties you behold,
And sing his name to harps of gold.
                              —ISAAC WATTS.

143   Soon may the last glad song.

1 Soon may the last glad song arise,
Through all the millions of the skies;
That song of triumph which records
That all the earth is now the Lord's.

2 Let thrones, and powers, and kingdoms be
Obedient, mighty God, to thee;
And over land, and stream, and main,
Now wave the scepter of thy reign.

3 O let that glorious anthem swell;
Let host to host the triumph tell,
Till not one rebel heart remains,
But over all the Saviour reigns.
                              —MRS. VOKE.

Hail, Thou Once Despised.

JOHN BAKEWELL.   Tune, AUTUMN. 8, 7, d.

1. Hail, thou once de-spis-ed Je - sus! Hail, thou Gal-i - le - an King!

Thou didst suf - fer to re-lease us; Thou didst free sal - va - tion bring.

D.S.—By thy mer - its we find fa - vor; Life is giv - en thro' thy name.

Fine.

D.S.

Hail, thou ag - o-niz-ing Sav-iour, Bearer of our sin and shame!

2 Paschal Lamb, by God appointed,
  All our sins on thee were laid:
By almighty love annointed,
  Thou hast full atonement made.
All thy people are forgiven,
  Through the virtue of thy blood;
Opened is the gate of heaven,
  Peace is made 'twixt man and God.

3 Jesus, hail! enthroned in glory,
  There forever to abide:
All the heavenly hosts adore thee,
  Seated at thy Father's side:
There for sinners thou art pleading:
  There thou dost our place prepare:
Ever for us interceding,
  Till in glory we appear.

4 Worship, honor, power, and blessing,
  Thou art worthy to receive;
Loudest praises, without ceasing,
  Meet it is for us to give.
Help, ye bright angelic spirits;
  Bring your sweetest, noblest lays;
Help to sing our Saviour's merits!
  Help to chant Immanuel's praise!

145   Love Divine.

1 Love divine, all love excelling,
  Joy of heaven, to earth come down!
Fix in us thy humble dwelling;
  All thy faithful mercies crown.
Jesus, thou art all compassion,
  Pure unbounded love thou art;
Visit us with thy salvation;
  Enter every trembling heart.

2 Come, almighty to deliver,
  Let us all thy life receive;
Suddenly return, and never,
  Never more thy temples leave:
Thee we would be always blessing,
  Serve thee as thy hosts above,
Pray, and praise thee without ceasing,
  Glory in thy perfect love.

3 Finish then thy new creation;
  Pure and spotless let us be;
Let us see thy great salvation,
  Perfectly restored in thee:
Changed from glory into glory,
  Till in heaven we take our place,
Till we cast our crowns before thee,
  Lost in wonder, love, and praise.
          —C. WESLEY.

Jesus, I my Cross have Taken.

HENRY F. LYTE. Tune, ELLESDIE. 8, 7, d.

1. Je- sus, I my cross have tak- en, All to leave and fol - low thee;

S: Na- ked, poor, despised, for- sak- en, Thou, from hence, my all shalt be:

D. S.—Yet how rich is my con- di - tion, God and heaven are still my own!

Fine.

D. S.

Per - ish ev - 'ry fond ambition, All I've sought and hoped, and known;

2 Let the world despise and leave me,
   They have left my Saviour, too;
Human hearts and looks deceive me;
   Thou art not, like man, untrue;
And, while thou shalt smile upon me,
   God of wisdom, love, and might,
Foes may hate, and friends may shun me;
   Show thy face, and all is bright.

3 Go, then, earthly fame and treasure!
   Come, disaster, scorn, and pain!
In thy service, pain is pleasure;
   With thy favor, loss is gain.
I have called thee, "Abba, Father;"
   I have stayed my heart on thee;
Storms may howl, and clouds may gather,
   All must work for good to me.

4 Man may trouble and distress me,
   'Twill but drive me to thy breast;
Life with trials hard may press me,
   Heaven will bring me sweeter rest.
O 'tis not in grief to harm me,
   While thy love is left to me;
O 'twere not in joy to charm me,
   Were that joy unmixed with thee.

5 Know, my soul, thy full salvation;
   Rise o'er sin, and fear, and care;
Joy to find in every station
   Something still to do or bear.

Think what Spirit dwells within thee;
   What a Father's smile is thine;
What a Saviour died to win thee:
   Child of heaven, shouldst thou repine?

6 Haste thee on from grace to glory,
   Armed by faith, and winged by prayer;
Heaven's eternal day's before thee,
   God's own hand shall guide thee there.
Soon shall close thy earthly mission,
   Swift shall pass thy pilgrim days,
Hope shall change to glad fruition,
   Faith to sight, and prayer to praise.

147   Gently Lead Us.

1 Gently, Lord, oh, gently lead us
   Through this lonely vale of tears,
Through the changes thou'st decreed us,
   Till our last great change appears;
When temptation's darts assail us,
   When in devious paths we stray,
Let thy goodness never fail us,
   Lead us in thy perfect way.

2 In the hour of pain and anguish,
   In the hour when death draws near,
Suffer not our hearts to languish,
   Suffer not our souls to fear;
And when mortal life is ended,
   Bid us in thine arms to rest,
Till by angel bands attended
   We awake among the blest.

—THOS. HASTINGS.

Glory to the Lamb.

Isaac Watts.   Wm. J. Kirkpatrick.

1. Come, let us join our cheer-ful songs With angels round the throne,
2. "Worthy the Lamb that died," they cry, "To be ex-alt-ed thus!"
3. Je-sus is wor-thy to re-ceive Hon-or and power di-vine;
4. The whole cre-a-tion join in one, To bless the sa-cred name

Ten thousand thousand are their tongues, But all their joys are one.
"Wor-thy the Lamb!" our hearts re-ply, "For he was slain for us."
And blessings more than we can give, Be, Lord, for-ev-er thine.
Of him that sits up-on the throne, And to a-dore the Lamb.

CHORUS.

Glo-ry to the Lamb! Glory to the Lamb! Glory to the bleeding Lamb!

Glo-ry to the Lamb! Glory to the Lamb! Glory to the bleeding Lamb!

Eternal Light!

BINNEY.

Tune, NEWCASTLE. 8, 6, 8, 8, 6.

1. Eternal light! eternal light! How pure the soul must be When, placed beneath thy

searching sight, It shrinks not, but with calm delight Can live, and look on thee!

2 The spirits that surround thy throne
May bear the burning bliss;
But that is surely their's alone,
Since they have never, never known
A fallen world like this.

3 Oh, how shall I, whose native sphere
Is dark, whose mind is dim,
Before the Ineffable appear,
And on my naked spirit bear
That uncreated beam?

4 There is a way for man to rise
To that sublime abode:—
An offering and a sacrifice,
A Holy Spirit's energies,
An Advocate with God:—

5 These, these prepare us for the sight
Of holiness above;
The sons of ignorance and night
May dwell in the Eternal Light
Through the Eternal Love!

150 Welcome, Sweet Day.

I. WATTS.

Tune, LISBON. S. M.

1. Welcome, sweet day of rest, That saw the Lord a - rise; Wel-
2. The King himself comes near, And feasts his saints to - day; Here

come to this re - viv - ing breast. And these re - joic - ing eyes!
we may sit, and see him here, And love, and praise, and pray.

3 One day in such a place,
Where thou, my God, art seen,
Is sweeter than ten thousand days
Of pleasurable sin.

4 My willing soul would stay
In such a frame as this,
And sit and sing herself away
To everlasting bliss.

151 **When all Thy Mercies.**

Joseph Addison.   Tune, MANOAH. C. M.

1. When all thy mer-cies, O my God, My ris-ing soul sur-veys,
2. Through hidden dangers, toils, and deaths, It gently cleared my way;

Transport-ed with the view, I'm lost In won-der, love, and praise.
And through the pleasing snares of vice, More to be feared than they.

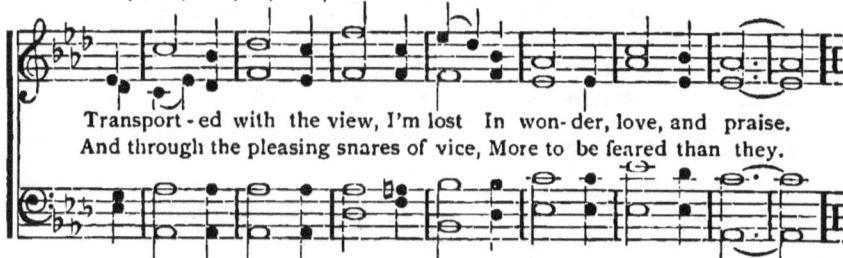

3 Through every period of my life
   Thy goodness I'll pursue;
   And after death, in distant worlds,
   The pleasing theme renew.

4 Through all eternity to thee
   A grateful song I'll raise;
   But oh, eternity's too short
   To utter all thy praise.

152 **How Sweet the Name.**

John Newton.   Tune, DOWNS. C. M.

1. How sweet the name of Je-sus sounds In a be-liev-er's ear!

It soothes his sor-rows, heals his wounds, And drives away his fear.

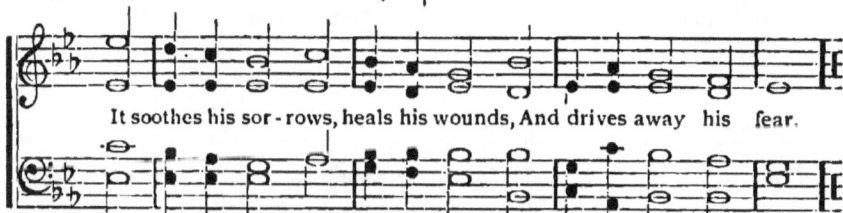

2 It makes the wounded spirit whole,
   And calms the troubled breast;
   'Tis manna to the hungry soul,
   And to the weary, rest.

3 Dear name! the rock on which I build,
   My shield and hiding-place;
   My never-failing treasure, filled
   With boundless stores of grace!

4 Jesus, my Shepherd, Saviour, Friend,
   My Prophet, Priest, and King,
   My Lord, my Life, my Way, my End,
   Accept the praise I bring!

5 I would thy boundless love proclaim
   With every fleeting breath;
   So shall the music of thy name
   Refresh my soul in death.

153 Watchman, Tell us of the Night.

Sir John Bowring.

Tune, WATCHMAN. 7s, d.

1. Watchman, tell us of the night, What its signs of promise are;

Traveler, o'er yon mountain's height See that glo-ry-beam-ing star!

Watchman, does its beauteous ray Aught of hope or joy for-tell?

Traveler, yes; it brings the day, Prom-ised day of Is-ra-el.

2 Watchman, tell us of the night;
  Higher yet that star ascends.
Traveler, blessedness and light,
  Peace and truth, its course portends!
Watchman, will its beams alone
  Gild the spot that gave them birth?
Traveler, ages are its own,
  See, it bursts o'er all the earth!

3 Watchman, tell us of the night,
  For the morning seems to dawn.
Traveler, darkness takes its flight;
  Doubt and terror are withdrawn.
Watchman, let thy wandering cease;
  Hie thee to thy quiet home!
Traveler, lo! the Prince of Peace,
  Lo! the Son of God is come!

154   The Lord's my Shepherd.   *Tune, DOWNS.*

1 The Lord's my Shepherd, I'll not want:
  He makes me down to lie
In pastures green; he leadeth me
  The quiet waters by.

2 My soul he doth restore again,
  And me to walk doth make
Within the paths of righteousness,
  E'en for his own name's sake.

3 Yea, though I walk through death's
  Yet will I fear no ill,   [dark vale,

For thou art with me, and thy rod
  And staff me comfort still.

4 A table thou hast furnished me
  In presence of my foes;
My head thou dost with oil anoint,
  And my cup overflows.

5 Goodness and mercy all my life
  Shall surely follow me,
And in God's house forevermore
  My dwelling-place shall be.

155 Go, Labor On.

H. Bonar.   Tune, MISSIONARY CHANT. L. M.

1. Go, la-bor on; spend and be spent, Thy joy to do the Fa-ther's will;

It is the way the Master went; Should not the servant tread it still?

2 Go, labor on; 'tis not for naught;
  Thine earthly loss is heavenly gain;
  Men heed thee, love thee, praise thee not;
  The Master praises,—what are men?

3 Go, labor on; your hands are weak;
  Your knees are faint, your soul cast
    down;
  Yet falter not; the prize you seek
  Is near,—a kingdom and a crown!

4 Toil on, faint not; keep watch, and pray!
  Be wise the erring soul to win;
  Go forth into the world's highway;
  Compel the wanderer to come in.

5 Toil on, and in thy toil rejoice;
  For toil comes rest, for exile home;
  Soon shalt thou hear the Bridegroom's
    voice,
  The midnight peal, "Behold, I come!"

156 Awake, my Soul.

P. Doddridge.   Tune, CHRISTMAS. C. M.

1. A-wake, my soul, stretch ev'ry nerve, And press with vigor on; A

heavenly race demands thy zeal, And an immortal crown, And an immortal crown.

2 A cloud of witnesses around
  Hold thee in full survey;
  Forget the steps already trod,
  And onward urge thy way.

3 'Tis God's all-animating voice
  That calls thee from on high;
  'Tis his own hand presents the prize
  To thine aspiring eye:—

4 That prize, with peerless glories bright,
  Which shall new luster boast,
  When victors' wreaths and monarchs'
    gems
  Shall blend in common dust. [gems

5 Blest Saviour, introduced by thee,
  Have I my race begun;
  And, crowned with victory, at thy feet
  I'll lay my honors down.

152

157 Eternal Beam of Light.

C. Wesley.

Tune, LOUVAN. L. M.

1. E - ter - nal Beam of light divine, Fountain of un - exhaust - ed love,
2. Je - sus, the wea - ry wanderer's rest, Give me thy ea - sy yoke to bear;

In whom the Father's glories shine, Thro' earth beneath, and heaven above;
With steadfast patience arm my breast, With spotless love and low - ly fear.

3 Thankful I take the cup from thee,
Prepared and mingled by thy skill;
Though bitter to the taste it be,
Powerful the wounded soul to heal.

4 Be thou, O Rock of Ages, nigh! [gone,
So shall each murmuring thought be
And grief, and fear, and care shall fly,
As clouds before the midday sun.

5 Speak to my warring passions, "Peace;"
Say to my trembling heart, "Be still;"
Thy power my strength and fortress is,
For all things serve thy sovereign will.

6 O Death! where is thy sting? where
Thy boasted victory, O Grave? [now
Who shall contend with God? or who
Can hurt whom God delights to save?

158 Blest be the Tie that Binds.

John Fawcett.

Tune, DENNIS. S. M.

1. Blest be the tie that binds Our hearts in Chris - tian love; The
2. Be - fore our Fa - ther's throne We pour our ar - dent prayers; Our

fel - low - ship of kind - red minds Is like to that a - bove.
fears, our hopes, our aims are one, Our com - forts and our cares.

3 We share our mutual woes,
Our mutual burdens bear;
And often for each other flows
The sympathizing tear.

4 When we asunder part,
It gives us inward pain;
But we shall still be joined in heart,
And hope to meet again.

159 The Hallowed Spot.

Rev. WM. HUNTER, D. D.

Arr. by T. C. O'KANE.

Fine.

1. { There is a spot to me more dear Than native vale or mountain;
A spot for which affection's tear Springs grateful from its fountain. }

D. S.—where I first my Saviour found, And felt my sins for-giv-en.

D. S.

'Tis not where kindred souls abound, Tho' that is al - most heaven, But

2 Hard was my toil to reach the shore,
Long tossed upon the ocean:
Above me was the thunder's roar,
Beneath the waves' commotion.
Darkly the pall of night was thrown
Around me, faint with terror;
In that dark hour how did my groan
Ascend for years of error.

3 Sinking and panting as for breath
I knew not help was near me;
I cried, "Oh, save me, Lord, from death,
Immortal Jesus, hear me;

Then quick as thought I felt him mine,
My Saviour stood before me;
I saw his brightness round me shine,
And shouted "Glory, glory."

4 O sacred hour! O hallowed spot!
Where love divine first found me;
Wherever falls my distant lot
My heart shall linger round thee.
And when from earth I rise, to soar
Up to my home in heaven,
Down will I cast my eyes once more,
Where I was first forgiven.

160 Thou Sweet, Gliding Kedron.

Arr. by J. J. HOOD.

[*Words on opposite page.*]

161 When for Eternal Worlds.

As sung by Wm. Hortz.

Arr. by W. J. K.

1. { When for e-ternal worlds I steer, And seas are calm and skies are clear, }
   { And faith in live-ly ex-er-cise, And distant hills of Canaan rise, }

2. { With cheerful hope her eyes explore Each landmark on the distant shore, }
   { The tree of life, the pastures green, The pearly gates, the crystal stream; }

My soul for joy then claps her wings, And loud her lovely sonnet sings, I'm
Again for joy she claps her wings, And loud her lovely sonnet sings, I'm

Fine.

D. S.

go-ing home, I'm go-ing home, And
al-most home, I'm almost home, A-

3
The nearer still she draws to land
More eager all her powers expand;
With steady helm and free bent sail,
Her anchor drops within the vale;
And now for joy she folds her wings,
‖: I'm safe at home, :‖
And her celestial sonnet sings,
I'm safe at home.

[*Music on opposite page.*]

1 Thou sweet, gliding Kedron, by thy silver stream,
  Our Saviour at midnight, when moonlight's pale beam
  Shone bright on thy waters, did frequently stray,
  And lose in thy murmurs the toils of the day.

2 How damp were the vapors that fell on his head,
  How hard was his pillow, how humble his bed!
  The angels, astonished, grew sad at the sight,
  And followed their Master with silent delight.

3 O garden of Olivet—dear, honored spot,
  The fame of thy wonders shall ne'er be forgot;
  The theme most transporting to seraphs above,
  The wonder of joy and the wonder of love.

4 Come, saints, and adore him, come, bow at his feet,
  Oh, give him the glory, the praise that is meet;
  Let joyful hosannas unceasing arise,
  And join the loud anthem that gladdens the skies.

162 Must Jesus Bear the Cross.

THOMAS SHEPHERD. Alt. Tune, MAITLAND. C. M.

1. Must Je - sus bear the cross a - lone, And all the world go free?

No, there's a cross for ev - 'ry one, And there's a cross for me.

2 How happy are the saints above,
Who once went sorrowing here!
But now they taste unmingled love,
And joy without a tear.

3 The consecrated cross I'll bear,
Till death shall set me free;
And then go home my crown to wear,
For there's a crown for me.

163 Blow ye the Trumpet.

C. WESLEY. Tune, LISCHER. H. M.

1. { Blow ye the trumpet, blow; The gladly solemn sound
Let all the nations know, To earth's remotest bound; } The year of jubilee is come:

2. { Jesus, our great High Priest, Hath full atonement made:
Ye weary spirits, rest; Ye mournful souls, be glad: } The year, etc.

Return, ye ransomed sinners, home, Return, ye ran - somed sinners, home.

3 Extol the Lamb of God,
The all-atoning Lamb;
Redemption in his blood
Throughout the world proclaim.

4 Ye slaves of sin and hell,
Your liberty receive,
And safe in Jesus dwell,
And blest in Jesus live.

5 Ye who have sold for naught
Your heritage above,
Shall have it back unbought,
The gift of Jesus' love.

6 The gospel trumpet hear,
The news of heavenly grace,
And saved from earth, appear
Before your Saviour's face.

156

O Glorious Hope.

Tune, WILLOUGHBY. C.P M.

1. O glorious hope of perfect love! It lifts me up to things above; It bears on eagles' wings;

It gives my ravished soul a taste, And makes me for some moments feast With Jesus' [priests and kings.

2 Rejoicing now in earnest hope,
I stand, and from the mountain top
See all the land below:
Rivers of milk and honey rise,
And all the fruits of paradise
In endless plenty grow.

3 A land of corn, and wine, and oil,
Favored with God's peculiar smile,
With every blessing blest; [ness,
There dwells the Lord our Righteous-
And keeps his own in perfect peace,
And everlasting rest.

4 O that I might at once go up;
No more on this side Jordan stop,
But now the land possess;
This moment end my legal years,
Sorrows and sins, and doubts and fears,
A howling wilderness!

165 Come on, my Partners.

1 Come on, my partners in distress,
My comrades through the wilderness,
Who still your bodies feel;
Awhile forget your griefs and fears,
And look beyond this vale of tears,
To that celestial hill.

2 Beyond the bounds of time and space,
Look forward to that heavenly place,
The saints' secure abode;
On faith's strong eagle pinions rise,
And force your passage to the skies,
And scale the mount of God.

3 Who suffer with our Master here,
We shall before his face appear
And by his side sit down;
To patient faith the prize is sure,
And all that to the end endure
The cross, shall wear the crown.

4 Thrice blessed, bliss-inspiring hope!
It lifts the fainting spirits up,
It brings to life the dead:
Our conflicts here shall soon be past,
And you and I ascend at last,
Triumphant with our Head.

5 That great mysterious Deity
We soon with open face shall see;
The beatific sight [praise,
Shall fill the heavenly courts with
And wide diffuse the golden blaze
Of everlasting light. —C. Wesley.

---

166   Welcome, Delightful Morn.   *Tune opposite.*

1 Welcome, delightful morn,
Thou day of sacred rest,
We hail thy kind return,
Lord, make these moments blest;
From the low train of mortal toys
We soar to reach immortal joys.

2 Now may the King descend
And fill his throne of grace;

Thy sceptre, Lord, extend,
While saints address thy face:
Let sinners feel thy quickening word,
And learn to know and fear the Lord.

3 Descend, celestial Dove!
With all thy quickening powers,
Disclose a Saviour's love,
And bless these sacred hours;
Then shall our souls new life obtain,
Nor Sabbaths be bestowed in vain.

167 C. Wesley. **Thou Hidden Source.** Tune, MARTILLO. 8s, 6l.

Fine.

1. Thou hidden source of calm repose, Thou all-suf-fi-cient love di-vine,
D. C.—And lo! from sin, and grief, and shame, I hide me, Je-sus, in thy name.

2. Thy mighty name sal-va-tion is, And keeps my happy soul a-bove:
D. C.—To me, with thy great name, are given Pardon, and ho-li-ness, and heaven.

D. C.

My help and refuge from my foes, Se-cure I am while thou art mine:
Comfort it brings, and power, and peace, And joy and ever-last-ing love:

3 Jesus, my all in all thou art;
  My rest in toil, my ease in pain;
  The medicine of my broken heart;
  In war, my peace; in loss, my gain;
  My smile beneath the tyrant's frown;
  In shame, my glory and my crown:

4 In want, my plentiful supply;
  In weakness, my almighty power;
  In bonds, my perfect liberty;
  My light, in Satan's darkest hour;
  In grief, my joy unspeakable;
  My life in death, my all in all.

168 C. Wesley. **Jesus hath Died.** Tune, AZMON. C. M.

1. Je-sus hath died that I might live, Might live to God a-lone;

In him e-ter-nal life re-ceive, And be in spir-it one.

2 Saviour, I thank thee for the grace,
  The gift unspeakable;
  And wait with arms of faith to embrace,
  And all thy love to feel.

3 My soul breaks out in strong desire
  The perfect bliss to prove;
  My longing heart is all on fire
  To be dissolved in love.

4 Give me thyself; from every boast,
  From every wish set free;
  Let all I am in thee be lost,
  But give thyself to me.

5 Thy gifts, alas! cannot suffice,
  Unless thyself be given;
  Thy presence makes my paradise,
  And where thou art is heaven.

INDEX.